S. Hrg. 105–743

YEAR 2000 LIABILITY AND DISCLOSURE

HEARING

BEFORE THE

SUBCOMMITTEE ON
FINANCIAL SERVICES AND TECHNOLOGY

OF THE

COMMITTEE ON
BANKING, HOUSING, AND URBAN AFFAIRS
UNITED STATES SENATE

ONE HUNDRED FIFTH CONGRESS

FIRST SESSION

ON

POTENTIAL FOR PROBLEMS RELATED TO YEAR 2000 COMPUTER CONVERSION AND NEED FOR DISCLOSURE

OCTOBER 22, 1997

Printed for the use of the Committee on Banking, Housing, and Urban Affairs

U.S. GOVERNMENT PRINTING OFFICE

52–579 CC   WASHINGTON : 1998

C O N T E N T S

ADDITIONAL MATERIAL SUPPLIED FOR THE RECORD

YEAR 2000 LIABILITY AND DISCLOSURE

WEDNESDAY, OCTOBER 22, 1997

U.S. SENATE,
COMMITTEE ON BANKING, HOUSING, AND URBAN AFFAIRS,
SUBCOMMITTEE ON FINANCIAL SERVICES AND TECHNOLOGY,
Washington, DC.

The Subcommittee met at 10:03 a.m., in room SD–538 of the Dirksen Senate Office Building, Senator Robert F. Bennett (Chairman of the Subcommittee) presiding.

OPENING STATEMENT OF SENATOR ROBERT F. BENNETT

Senator BENNETT. The Subcommittee will come to order.

We're holding another hearing today on the Year 2000 computer problem. The first time we held a hearing, everyone said, this is useful. Maybe we ought to have another one. That's a little bit unusual in Washington. Usually, you hold one hearing and the matter then automatically and magically goes away, until you produce some legislation.

After holding a second hearing it became apparent that this is going to be a larger problem than we thought. We then decided to hold this hearing.

We have learned in the previous hearings that the Year 2000 problem is more than just a computer problem; it is a pervasive business issue for which there is clearly no quick-fix. Businesses in today's world rely on computer systems for virtually every aspect of their operation, from running elevators to calculating interest on loans, to launching satellites. A failure in one computer system could not only devastate the operation it controls, but could also domino through other systems and cause other seemingly unrelated operations to shut down. As a result, virtually every business in this country will face a stream of potential direct and contingent liabilities based on the failures of their own systems or those of their business partners.

After the first hearing, I went to a board meeting of a company on whose board I am allowed to sit, the only one that I am allowed to sit on under Senate ethics rules, and as a Director, raised this issue with the managers of that particular business, do we have a Year 2000 problem?

They quickly responded that, no, we don't. And based on the information in the hearing, I didn't believe them. They convinced me, however—this is a relatively new company and they said, because virtually every one of our software programs has been developed in the last 5 years, the software is all new enough that the Year 2000 problem is not embedded in it. And I took that at face value.

I am now going to go back to them and say, let's take a look at your hardware and see if there are some Year 2000 problems in the hardware that you may have overlooked.

I tell this to indicate that business managers need to be aware of the costs and exposures connected with the Year 2000 problem. Directors need to be asking these kinds of questions in their own board meetings because if it turns up that a company has a serious Year 2000 problem that will cost a sufficient amount of money to fix, the question of disclosure to shareholders raises its head and the question of liability on the part of management to fail to disclose raises its head, and these are issues that we are going to be discussing in this morning's hearing.

How big an issue is this part of the Year 2000 problem?

Estimates that have come before me indicate that litigation costs for companies as a result of the Year 2000 problem could run as high as a trillion dollars. This is one-seventh of the total size of the economy for an issue on which there is no rate of return on the amount of money that you spend. There is no advantage in terms of increased productivity or anything else. Despite this incredible figure, individual companies are not talking about the specific liabilities they face or how they plan to manage their litigation risk. They are being silent, and that silence raises two important questions that we plan to pursue in this morning's hearing.

First, what should individual companies be doing to identify and manage their Year 2000 litigation risks and what, if anything, can the Federal Government do to help them?

If there is, indeed, more than a trillion dollars worth of litigation lurking in the next century, what should individual companies be doing to either identify or, hopefully, eliminate that particular risk?

Few companies have been able to determine whether they have that exposure and to what extent they are vulnerable. Companies that are unable to determine their specific risks will not be able to manage them and certainly, will not properly disclose them to the public and thereby, will increase their risks.

That leads to the second, and perhaps more important question. Should individual companies be required by law to disclose the projected expenditure and legal and operational uncertainties associated with their Year 2000 remediation efforts?

When I say, by law, I include, of course, regulations from the SEC. Or, in the banking world, by the various regulators.

Is this a safety and soundness issue that should be disclosed to investors, either potential or existing shareholders?

Is this a balance sheet item for which reserves should be set up on the part of businesses outside of the financial services areas that would affect earnings per share in a material way?

I believe that investors have a right to know what type and amount of risk individual companies face as a result of the Year 2000 problem. My staff has conducted a review of the 10–K's published on the SEC's EDGAR database which reveals that very few companies have made any specific disclosures with regard to the Year 2000 problem. Most of the disclosures that have been made state generally that the companies are spending money on the problem, no real specifics and quantification. Despite the enormous projected litigation figures, companies are not reporting their specific exposure or setting up reserves with which to deal with that.

The SEC has recently issued a legal interpretation recommending that companies properly disclose the legal and operational risks and the uncertainties relating to the Year 2000 problem, and I look forward to the SEC's testimony on how they plan to enforce this interpretation. But I question whether a legal interpretation is sufficient to encourage companies to make appropriate disclosures.

It may well be that some stronger action, perhaps in the form of legislation, is necessary to require, rather than simply encourage, companies to keep investors informed. Such a law could require companies to disclose, on an ongoing basis, the projected expenditures and legal and operational uncertainties connected with their Year 2000 remediation efforts. This type of law would help ensure that the investors and the general public are made aware of the progress of remediation efforts within U.S. companies and the direct and contingent liabilities that those companies face.

I think every investor has a right to those facts. I have the right to them as a Director, asking the question in the company where I serve. But certainly the shareholders that I represent as a Director have an equal right.

It is the responsibility and the burden of the company to disclose those facts and it is unfair and unrealistic to expect an individual investor or an individual depositor at a financial institution to try to dig out those inquiries and information on their own.

Now with that much of a doomsday kind of scenario, we turn to today's panel of witnesses to help us solve the problem, lead us through the thicket and turn doomsday into sunshine.

Our first panel, we welcome back Jeff Jinnett, President of the LeBoeuf Computing Technologies. He serves as Of Counsel to the New York law firm of LeBoeuf, Lamb, Greene & MacRae. He has written extensively on the Year 2000 topics and has appeared, as I said, before the Subcommittee earlier this year. The rest of the panel consists of Dana McDaniel, Chairman of the Technology and Intellectual Property Section in the law firm of Williams, Mullen, Christian & Dobbins in Richmond, Virginia, and Harris Miller, President of the Information Technology Association of America. We welcome you two gentlemen as well.

These witnesses will discuss the potential liability companies face as a result of the Year 2000 problem and, I hope, offer some recommendations for Congress as to what can be done to help answer my second question.

Gentlemen, I welcome you on behalf of the Subcommittee.

Mr. Jinnett, we will start with you first.

OPENING STATEMENT OF JEFF JINNETT
PRESIDENT, LeBOEUF COMPUTING TECHNOLOGIES, L.L.C.
AND OF COUNSEL, LeBOEUF, LAMB, GREENE & MacRAE, L.L.P.

Mr. JINNETT. Mr. Chairman, distinguished Members of the Subcommittee, my name is Jeff Jinnett and I am President of LeBoeuf Computing Technologies, a business subsidiary of the law firm of LeBoeuf, Lamb, Greene & MacRae of which law firm I was formerly a Partner and now serve as Of Counsel. I appreciate the opportunity to again testify before this Subcommittee.

Over the past year, I have consulted with numerous large corporations in the financial services industry. For the most part, these corporations are quite confident that they will successfully complete their Year 2000 remediation efforts and make their internal computer systems fully Year 2000 compliant. However, many of these large corporations are concerned about their operations being disrupted by Year 2000 system failures of smaller business partners who have fewer resources to devote to their Y2K compliance efforts.

An additional risk these financial institutions may not have considered is that they may become defendants in litigation brought against their smaller business partners where the cause of the business partner's computer system failures is unclear. Due to the applicable statutes of limitation and the desire of the plaintiffs to seek joint and several liability from all defendants in case the primary defendant files for bankruptcy, the plaintiff's attorneys are likely to sue not only the primary defendant, but also any business partner which conceivably could have played a part in the computer system failure due to the sharing of noncompliant data or software. Companies should be mindful that such a trial can become a very expensive battle of conflicting expert witnesses.

If at the time of the trial, the Year 2000 computer problem has resulted in serious personal injuries in the society at large due to malfunctioning hospital equipment, air traffic control systems, or has resulted in higher unemployment due to increased corporate bankruptcies, some juries may be predisposed to the plaintiff's position and be inclined to award punitive damages to send a message to corporate America. Plaintiff's counsel may also point out that the Y2K problem has been known for decades and yet the defendant did not begin actual corrective work until late in the 1990's, arguing that this is evidence of a reckless disregard for the problem. Plaintiff's counsel may say to the jury, "After all, it's only a matter of going from two digits to four digits. How hard can that be? There must be gross negligence here."

In light of the above potential scenario, financial institutions should take all necessary steps to create a due-diligence record which could be introduced into evidence in litigation, if necessary, to show that the enterprise acted in good faith, using commercially reasonable efforts to solve its Year 2000 problem.

Financial institutions should adopt a comprehensive risk management approach to the Year 2000 problem, rather than merely a technical remediation approach. For example, the enterprise should review its Year 2000 corrective plan against currently available industry metrics as to remediation and testing costs and methods in order to confirm that the plan adopted by the enterprise matches the current industry best practices. As part of this effort, the enterprise could seek to obtain certification of its Year 2000 corrective plan under the ITAA*2000 program, as was recently done by BankBoston.

Dr. Edward Yardeni, the Chief Economist with Deutsche Morgan Grenfell, has estimated that a recession may occur by the Year 2000 due, in part, to the Year 2000 computer problem. In light of the complexity of the Y2K problem and the potentially severe impact it may have on the U.S. economy, it is advisable that financial institutions be encouraged to share information as to Year 2000 compliance status, remediation techniques which they have found helpful and Y2K technical, business and legal risks which they discovered may impact other financial institutions. However, due to fears of providing plaintiffs' attorneys with litigation ammunition, financial institutions may be reluctant to engage in industry-wide Y2K information-sharing efforts. This fear of litigation exposure is heightened due to the potential imposition of punitive damages on defendants.

In order to encourage financial institutions to become fully compliant and to share necessary information with other institutions, I recommend that this Subcommittee consider introducing legislation to provide a safe harbor from punitive damages for financial institutions which establish that they have made a good faith effort to become Year 2000 compliant and which cooperate with industry-wide sharing of Y2K information as may be requested by appropriate regulatory authorities. The demonstration of a good faith effort to become Year 2000 compliant could be made by a national bank, for example, by passing a Year 2000 compliancy audit conducted by the Office of the Comptroller of the Currency. For financial institutions where no Federal regulatory authority has planned to conduct extensive Y2K audits, a quasi-governmental entity could be established by Congress to conduct the audits.

A strong case can be made that punitive damages are inappropriate in Y2K litigation, in any event. Punitive damages are imposed upon reprehensible conduct and to deter others from similar behavior in the future. This simply does not apply to the Year 2000 computer problem. As Dr. Leon Kappelman has demonstrated, the use by programmers of two digits rather than four digits in year date fields was necessary in past years to save expensive computer memory. Dr. Kappelman calculates that over the past 35 years, companies have saved far more in computer memory costs than they will spend on Y2K remediation and, therefore, the use of two digits rather than four digits for year date fields constituted good business judgment. The Y2K problem did not arise from reprehensible conduct. Further, since the Y2K problem is a one-time occurrence, imposing punitive damages on an individual defendant in Y2K litigation will not serve any deterrence function whatsoever, either with respect to the specific defendant or to other potential defendants.

Additional aspects of a Y2K litigation safe harbor could be considered, including the prohibition of liability for noneconomic pain and suffering losses, and the elimination of joint and several liability in favor of a proportionate liability standard.

In conclusion, the Year 2000 computer problem poses significant litigation risks for many financial services institutions, not necessarily because they themselves will fail to become Year 2000 compliant, but because they may be affected by the failures of third-party business partners to become fully Year 2000 compliant. As a critical part of the U.S. infrastructure, the financial services industry must become Year 2000 compliant if severe disruptions to the economy are to be avoided. If financial institutions adopt a comprehensive Y2K risk management approach rather than merely a technical remediation approach, they should be better able to identify and reduce their technical, business, and legal Y2K risks, not only as individual institutions, but also as an industry. In this effort, open disclosure by financial institutions of Y2K compliancy status to their counterpart financial partners, sharing of remediation techniques, and other information-sharing would aid in the industry-wide Y2K effort.

The financial industry's justifiable concerns over attracting punitive damage awards due to such disclosures makes it imperative that Congress consider enacting legislation creating a Y2K litigation safe harbor shielding financial institutions from excessive litigation risks, provided the institutions make a good faith effort to become Year 2000 compliant and to participate in industry-wide sharing of Y2K information, as requested by appropriate regulatory authorities.

Mr. Chairman and Members of the Subcommittee, that concludes my testimony and I would be pleased to answer any questions.

Senator BENNETT. Thank you very much.

Mr. McDaniel.

OPENING STATEMENT OF DANA D. McDANIEL, CHAIRMAN TECHNOLOGY AND INTELLECTUAL PROPERTY SECTION WILLIAMS, MULLEN, CHRISTIAN & DOBBINS

Mr. McDANIEL. Thank you, Senator.

Mr. Chairman, Members of the Subcommittee, thank you for inviting me here to testify today.

As a commercial trial lawyer advising clients every day with respect to liability and remediation issues arising out of the Year 2000 computer problem, I will spend my time briefly addressing three areas of legal liability that are of concern to businesses. Those are—contract liability, statutory liability to consumers, and liability to shareholders.

I will conclude by suggesting further study of two issues. First, a clarifying amendment to Section 117 of the Copyright Act; and, second, concurring with Mr. Jinnett, the further study of possible safe harbor legislation, especially with respect to Federal consumer protection laws which provide for the recovery of attorneys' fees and statutory damages.

Contract liability will arise in relationships up and down the supply and the distribution chain when Year 2000 problems cause manufacturing, ordering, delivery, and accounting systems to malfunction. While the potential for those problems is real and significant, current law adequately allocates the resulting liability among the parties. Under current law, in the absence of contractual limitations, losses caused by Year 2000 failures should ultimately fall on the party in breach.

We believe that there is no reason to alter that outcome in the context of a contract breach caused by a Year 2000 problem. To do so, would shift the risk of loss caused by Year 2000 problems to a nonbreaching party, with little or no ability to avoid that loss.

There is no compelling reason to alter existing law to reach this result in Year 2000-related cases. Moreover, this outcome provides a strong incentive for parties to ensure that they and their upstream counterparties become Year 2000 compliant in time to avoid such a breach.

Our assessment of contract liability, therefore, is that while the potential for such claims is significant, competitive forces and existing law are adequate and no specialized legislation is needed in that area.

With respect to statutory liability to consumers, mass consumer-based businesses, including the financial services industry, risk both causing and suffering the greatest disruption from Year 2000 computer problems. Most of this disruption, however, is likely to be temporary, and while frustrating to consumers is not likely to cause substantial economic damage.

In those instances when consumers suffer damages, State law remedies are available, and given the nature of likely consumer claims—that is, that they should be high in number, similar in nature, but small in individual dollar amount—State attorney general and private class actions offer consumers effective remedies. Special purpose legislation creating additional consumer protection or causes of action specifically related to Year 2000 computer problems does not appear to us to be either necessary or desirable.

With respect to shareholder liability, it is certainly not unreasonable to expect that either internal or external Year 2000 computer problems will adversely affect the share price, value or viability of some publicly traded and closely held corporations. As a result, shareholders may have viable statutory and/or common law claims against corporate directors and officers who failed to exercise due care in addressing this issue.

Under current law and applicable regulations, disclosure and prudent management remain the best deterrents and defenses to shareholder derivative and similar suits. We, therefore, again believe that existing law adequately establishes the obligations of officers and directors to disclose reasonably anticipated Year 2000 problems and to protect shareholders' interests with respect to those problems.

In each of these areas—contract liability, consumer liability, and shareholder liability—we believe current law is sufficient and that the Year 2000 problem does not create any need for broad, specialized legislation. It seems to us that the Year 2000 issue is one in which bad or unique facts could make bad or unique law. Legislation enacted specifically to address Year 2000 computer problems is likely to yield awkward results and disruptive legal precedent. That said, however, I do recommend further study of two issues.

First, I believe Congress should consider a clarifying amendment to Section 117 of the Copyright Act, which presently authorizes licensees of computer programs to make certain adaptations to those programs under certain specified circumstances.

Many companies seeking to remediate Year 2000 deficiencies face uncertainties because the Copyright Act does not clearly authorize them to employ self-help to remediate those deficiencies.

Vendors claim that users are precluded under their license agreements from modifying software to make it Year 2000 ready. The necessary modifications do not fall clearly within either the Act's definition of fair use, under Section 107, or its definition of a permissible adaptation of a computer program under Section 117. This uncertainty raises two problems that we face every day.

One, remediation contractors are refusing to modify any software product without authorization from the software vendor.

Two, many vendors exploit this uncertainty by refusing to grant licenses to permit this work or conditioning such a license on the vendor receiving a release from Year 2000 liability. Some vendors can't be located, others are nonresponsive to a request for a license, and even others respond with claims that they will be ready, but without concrete evidence to support those claims.

While one could argue that Section 107, which defines fair use, and Section 117, which authorizes certain adaptations of computer programs, permit in-house remediation, they do not clearly do so and there is no controlling legal precedent.

End users and Year 2000 remediation vendors are understandably reluctant to become the legal test case for these theories and, in any event, the judicial process is unlikely to resolve the issue in time to be helpful. The unfairness this situation creates is at odds with the balance Congress sought to strike between the rights of owners of computer copyrights and their users, and leaves users in an impossible position.

One way Congress could remedy this situation is by modifying Section 117 of the Copyright Act to include within the statutory definition of a permissible adaptation, modifications necessary to correct Year 2000 deficiencies. And I would note that a limitation on Section 117's right to make adaptations is that they cannot be exploited for further commercial purposes.

Second, we also suggest, in concurrence with Mr. Jinnett, that a study be undertaken with respect to possible safe harbor legislation. What we are hearing from large corporations is the concern of pervasive consumer complaints where, in the situation where there has been a technical violation of a Federal consumer protection statute. We believe it may be appropriate to exempt technical violations of those laws and regulations caused by Year 2000 problems in cases in which the violations cause little or no actual economic harm. Any such protection could be conditioned upon the business' good faith pursuit and implementation of the Year 2000 remediation plan.

The point, however, is that if lawyers perceive violations of statutes which provide for recovery of statutory damages and/or attorney's fees, one can easily foresee that the $1-trillion prediction could, in fact, occur. However, much can be done from a legislative standpoint in that regard to ensure that outcome does not occur.

In conclusion, the ultimate goal of this Subcommittee and those of us involved in the Year 2000 issue is to minimize the effect of the Year 2000 problem on local, national, and international commerce. The threat of legal liability has compelled corporate America to acknowledge and address this issue much more aggressively than most of our international counterparts. Still, major U.S. corporations are just now fully committing to remediate this problem and it can be assumed that smaller businesses will soon follow suit.

While publicizing this issue through hearings like this and press coverage will go a long way toward informing businesses of the need for Year 2000 remediation, we do not believe at this time that it is appropriate to enact legislation that would relieve the pressures created by our current legal system unless those pressures present a threat that is unfair, as in the case of the Copyright Act anomaly, or unproductive, as in the case of consumer actions that are driven more by the prospect of recovering attorneys' fees than by any legitimate harm to consumers.

We, therefore, do not propose any significant special purpose legislation specifically targeting the Year 2000 computer problem at this time. We do propose further study of the two issues that I mentioned, and that this situation should be monitored for further overall study.

Thank you, Mr. Chairman.

Senator BENNETT. Thank you very much.

Mr. Miller.

OPENING STATEMENT OF HARRIS N. MILLER
PRESIDENT, INFORMATION TECHNOLOGY ASSOCIATION
OF AMERICA (ITAA)

Mr. MILLER. Good morning. I am Harris Miller, President of the Information Technology Association of America, which represents 11,000 direct and affiliate member companies in the information technology industry. ITAA members are the marketplace leaders in a host of critical information technology areas, including product and custom software, telecommunications, Internet, systems integration, and outsourcing.

Chairman Bennett, ITAA applauds your outstanding leadership on this Year 2000 issue. The challenge we face in rising to this issue is enormous, a challenge which hits the banking and financial industry particularly hard because of several factors. These include the information-sensitive, date-sensitive nature of its business; the forward-looking orientation of the banking industry's operations; the immediate effect this situation could have on typical consumers; the risks involved in lending money to potentially unprepared customers; the growing reliance on electronic commerce offerings to gain competitive advantage; the need to interconnect with a wide variety of trading partners, both in this country and abroad; and, last but not least, the enormous importance this industry represents to the national and to the global economies.

ITAA supports the efforts of this Subcommittee because this is where the rubber meets the road. It will be through the efforts of this Subcommittee and others focused on key industry sectors that Year 2000 will receive the attention it deserves. We encourage similar hearings in such areas as transportation, public health, energy, defense, and other aspects of modern society.

ITAA is concerned about the Year 2000 status of both the national and the international banking systems. While some national banks have staked out the high ground on this issue, we are concerned that there are many banks and financial services firms which still remain silent on their Year 2000 preparedness. Even banks which have a Year 2000 program may be slow to translate their plans into action. I am concerned that banks, like many other types of firms, are victims of analysis paralysis—the disabling disease which inhibits the ability of organizations to admit that business survival is the real issue with the Year 2000, that mistakes will inevitably happen, and that tough choices must be made now. It's time to make those choices and move on.

From the international banking perspective, our dealings with foreign bankers suggest a disturbing degree of inaction. We hear similar concerns voiced by other observers as well.

Today, I have been asked to testify about ITAA's Year 2000 certification program called ITAA*2000, which Mr. Jinnett referenced. I'm delighted to do so because we have a very positive story to tell.

ITAA has been engaged for several years, Mr. Chairman, in educating governments at all levels, the private sector, and the international community about the actions necessary to address the Year 2000 issue and the very real risks of inaction. Last year, our Year 2000 Task Force, comprised of over one hundred companies, approved the idea of a Year 2000 certification program. While ITAA*2000 offers a substantive, rigorous technical evaluation of applicants, the program should be properly viewed from a strategic business vantage point.

The topic of this hearing is liability. The focus of our program is to provide a mechanism by which organizations are able to mitigate the downstream risk associated with this work.

Other goals behind our program are: First, to give the marketplace a mechanism to identify the best-of-breed companies in addressing the Year 2000 issue. Second, to address a growing sense of concern within Federal agencies and a viewpoint articulated by other people in Government that IT companies are not doing enough to respond to the Y2K compliance concerns of their customers. Third, to take a proactive, industry-based stance on the Year 2000 issue, partially in response to a request made by your colleague, Congressman Stephen Horn, in the first Congressional hearing on this issue, in April 1996.

Our ITAA*2000 program was developed in conjunction with the Software Productivity Consortium based in Herndon, VA, which has a great deal of expertise in software process improvement. The Consortium provides the technical manpower to staff our program, which we publicly announced October 1, 1996.

The program has grown to become the widely acknowledged industry certification program, something of a standard. Today, 45 organizations have received certification, with another 12 in process. In fact, Mr. Chairman, we will be announcing three more certifications this week. Several other companies have informed us they expect to submit completed applications shortly.

Let me talk about one recent program graduate which could be of particular interest to you and this Subcommittee. Last month, BankBoston received ITAA*2000 certification. As you know, Bank Boston is one of the Nation's leading financial institutions in working its way through the Year 2000 thicket. As early as December 1996, we reported in our weekly *Year 2000 Outlook* on the impressive progress BankBoston was making with its 40-million-plus lines of code. A representative from that company has testified before your Subcommittee.

In gaining ITAA*2000 certification, BankBoston was able to demonstrate that it had a set of formal methods in place in 11 areas critical to its success, from initial assessment to final testing. Bank Boston is the first financial institution to gain the Year 2000 certification distinction and we hope that many others will follow.

Almost 350 companies have requested the questionnaire necessary to go through the certification process. Frankly, we are somewhat perplexed by why more completed questionnaires have not yet been submitted. Let me hazard some guesses.

First, the application process is very rigorous, perhaps more rigorous than some companies are willing to go through. Completed applications are often several inches thick. We do not issue these certifications lightly and several organizations have failed the review. And perhaps some fail themselves, starting the process assuming that our certification program is merely pro forma, and having second thoughts when they realize the challenge of becoming certified.

Let me discuss in some detail how the program actually works.

Applicants such as BankBoston respond to an in-depth technical questionnaire, provide extensive documentation, and respond to extensive follow-up questions and requests for further information.

The focus of the review, Mr. Chairman, is on the processes and methods that organizations use to develop the Year 2000 compliance software. To date, most of the program graduates have been information technology companies, but the program is designed to apply to any company, Government agency, or other entity involved in the Year 2000 conversion. The certification can involve organizations which sell products or services commercially, but it's also of equal interest to those developing systems for internal use only. It requires an independent, third-party review of Year 2000 processes and methods.

Our thinking, Mr. Chairman, very simply, is that if you get the processes and methods right on the front end, you dramatically reduce the chances of failure down the road. This concept of reviewing processes and methods is very similar to the ISO 9000 process which is widely used in our industry and other industries which try to set the highest standards.

An organization which goes through our certification process successfully demonstrates to its customers, business partners, stockholders, and other interested parties that, well in advance of the century rollover, they have understood the Year 2000 problem, taken the best possible steps to correct it, and in so doing, met the industry's best practices for dealing with the Year 2000 issue.

Does that guarantee that software will operate flawlessly in the years to come? Of course not. No single program could hold itself out as the ultimate arbiter of Year 2000 compliance. There are simply too many platforms, systems, languages, interfaces, and other date-dependent components to check and not enough time. Every organization's computing environment is sui generis. Attempting to recreate such environments on a customer-by-customer basis is just a bridge too far.

A Year 2000 solution that works well in one computing environment may not work very well at all in another. It simply would be impossible for our certification program or any other to test all possible environments in all possible interface situations.

The ITAA*2000 certification program, as strong as we believe it is, cannot be a substitute for an organization's own verification program. For the reasons I just mentioned, we believe companies should tailor a Year 2000 verification program which is right for them—incorporating company methods and practices, identifying key interfaces, setting testing criteria, and putting the management practices in place to ensure compliance. Part of this internal program should include steps to ensure Year 2000 compliance by its hardware and software vendors, and others with products using microprocessors or programmable logic controllers.

To this end, ITAA companies have developed a standard questionnaire for customer use in communicating with their suppliers. Our purpose is two-fold—to help customers ask the right questions of their vendors and to help the vendors deal with the many thousands of contacts they receive on the issue, all asking for the same basic information in multiple ways.

Speaking as an industry executive, I am proud that our association has stepped up to the Year 2000 certification challenge. ITAA *2000 is only one of several Year 2000 initiatives we have underway, including seminars, a Year 2000 directory, a buyer's guide, and a weekly Internet-based newsletter which we distribute at no cost. We have been very active in trying to get other industry and industry groups informed about the Year 2000 challenge. I am pleased to report we have built a collaborative Year 2000 program with the National Retail Federation. We have also worked with other associations, such as the Securities Industry Association and the Automotive Industry Action Council. We have also been active conference presenters on this topic across the country.

We have also been involved in our educational program and our ITAA*2000 certification program overseas. My staff and I have given seminars around the world, including China, Singapore, Canada, France, Brazil, Mexico, Hong Kong and soon, Argentina. In all of these areas, certification is a topic of interest.

I also serve as President of the World Information Technology and Services Alliance, which is comprised of 29 IT associations from around the world like ours. This association has adopted its own Year 2000 policy paper calling for an increased global focus on the Year 2000 challenge. ITAA has signed several agreements with our global sister associations to offer our certification program in their countries.

In conclusion, Mr. Chairman, we believe that the certification program helps to address the liability issue. Thank you very much, and I would be glad to respond to any questions you have about our program.

Senator BENNETT. Thank you. This has been very informative, all three of you.

Senator Grams, do you have a comment or statement?

OPENING COMMENT OF SENATOR ROD GRAMS

Senator GRAMS. I don't have an opening statement. I just want to commend you for holding this hearing. I know it is very important and I am really looking forward to hearing some of the information. So, basically, I am here as an observer, to absorb, rather than to say anything.

Thank you, Mr. Chairman.

Senator BENNETT. Very good. Thank you.

Here is a scenario that has been called to my attention. Let's take BankBoston, which has been very open and public about this.

This may or may not apply to them, but theoretically, let's say that a bank has done as much as BankBoston has done with respect to solving its own problems. Along the way someone says, that's fine, but what about correspondent banks or other major customers who may not be Year 2000 compliant and whose problems may spill over into your systems and cause significant difficulty?

Then some executive with the compliant bank says, let's send out a list of recommendations to all of our customers, telling them the things that they ought to be doing, in order to help them with their Year 2000 problem. That seems to be a fairly logical kind of service for the bank to render to its customers.

At which point, someone shows up from Mr. Jinnett's law firm counseling the bank and says, if you do that, you're opening yourself up for all kinds of liability claims, because let's say you list 15 handy steps of things that should be done to make yourself Year 2000 compliant, and inadvertently leave off No. 16, which could have made a significant difference.

In a courtroom, in the year 2001, or whenever the lawsuit finally comes before the judge, assuming they got the elevators fixed in the courthouse——

[Laughter.]

—the plaintiff attorney says, we complied with all 15 of the items listed in the bank's recommendations, and we still fell short. Therefore, it is the bank's responsibility for our failure because they didn't add number 16.

Under advice from a lawyer that the failure to list every possible circumstance, the bank then does nothing. It doesn't send out even the first 15 because they don't want the liability of not including number 16.

That may give them some relief legally from the legal exposure, but it stops a procedure that would go a long way toward solving the problem, and therefore, is not good in the marketplace for the bank to take that defensive posture.

That's the scenario that's been presented to me. Comments on it? Is it a legitimate thing to be concerned about? Should we make, Mr. McDaniel, some kind of legal changes that would allow banks to have a safe harbor to disclose that kind of information? Are the lawyers, Mr. Jinnett, going to react in the way I have described? Let's have a discussion about that one.

Mr. McDaniel. Well, I would just have a further question about the hypothetical. And that is, in giving the list of 15 steps, is the bank's purpose to instruct the client on how to become compliant in interfacing with the bank's system, or has the bank undertaken the larger effort of informing the client how to become Year 2000 compliant, because, as a lawyer, I would certainly instruct my client not to take that step, but, rather, to limit its communications with customers to those steps necessary to interface appropriately and properly with the bank in this instance.

Assuming that is the case, then I believe that a plaintiff's lawyer would be hard pressed to turn the missing element into a significant legal loophole or foothold if the only disruption is to the client's relationship with the bank. That is certainly how I would advise my clients.

Now if the bank is insistent on taking the larger step, or if, in instructing the client how to interface with the bank, the bank must necessarily effect further interfaces downstream, then we would need to visit that issue significantly before coming up with the list of 15. I still, however, as you might have heard in my comments, am resistant to broad legislation addressed to that issue.

The bank's obligations to its clients and the client's obligations to the bank are already part of a fully negotiated contractual relationship that should be preserved and not redrafted. If the bank is attempting to be helpful with respect to that relationship, it is hard for me to foresee the real prospect of meaningful lender liability claims, et cetera.

Senator BENNETT. Other comments?

Mr. MILLER. I will let the lawyer talk first.

Mr. JINNETT. I encountered some clients that are more conservative than that. What they do is send out awareness letters to their correspondents trying to heighten the awareness of the problem, encouraging them to become Year 2000 compliant, and then saying that they would like to run tests with the correspondent entity to make sure that their systems interface well with the host system.

So, they in writing will not tell them the 15 things they need to do to interface with the host system. They will just say, you need to become compliant, and then let's run a test with our two systems to make sure that we are interfacing correctly.

They are very concerned about leaving a smoking gun in the file where they may be seen as instructing another party as to what it takes to interface with their system and, falling short, they may have missed something.

Senator BENNETT. Mr. Miller.

Mr. MILLER. This is an issue that our association, frankly, deals with all the time because some of our members have said, that because our association has taken the lead—in fact, we are the only information technology association talking about Year 2000 on a regular basis—either we are brilliant or we are crazy. The concern is that some day, someone's going to come back and say, well, ITAA played this leadership role, and we are going to become the object of all kinds of lawsuits down the road.

Senator BENNETT. Yes.

Mr. MILLER. Either the association or our certification program. The conclusion of our board of directors was this issue was simply too important not to engage in an active awareness campaign.

We try our best to indicate to our audiences, whether it be a bank or any other organization, that at the end of the day, they must test, they must implement, and they must verify. Whatever steps we suggest or any vendor we refer them to, at the end of the day, they don't make any sense unless the system actually works.

But I certainly, without commenting on the specific question, would have to defer to the lawyers as to what changes need to be in the law. On the other hand, I think that financial institutions, insurance companies, and others have to play a key role in this awareness campaign, particularly for the small- and medium-sized businesses.

Everyone agrees that the biggest concerns that industry observers have about Year 2000 compliance is not with the bigger companies. The feeling is that ultimately, they have the money and the resources, and even if they panic at the last minute, they will get it done somehow. But it is the small- and medium-sized enterprises which are most at risk. How do you get their attention? For a small- or medium-sized business which is struggling to make payroll and to recruit enough workers and everything else, how do you get their attention on the Year 2000?

Well, if your banker says, we are going to pull your line of credit, and your insurance company says, we are not going to continue to insure you, those are the kinds of incentives that will get even the small- and medium-sized business to pay attention.

Exactly how that awareness letter from the bank is worded to address the legitimate concerns that Mr. McDaniel raised, that is up to that insurance company or that bank to decide with their legal counsel. But for the banks not to do anything, or an insurance company not to do anything because they're afraid that they might become ultimately a plaintiff in a lawsuit, I think would be very unfortunate.

These are the people, these are the types of industries that can really influence their customers, whether it is a mom and pop shop or a multibillion-dollar corporation. They can influence those people, the CEO's of those smaller companies, by saying, you are not doing enough. If a company says, "We just got a letter from our bank, we just got a letter from our insurance company," that company will pay attention. That company will say, "I want to make sure that we're doing enough. Otherwise, when I get back from my annual review from my insurance or my banker, we're not going to be in business any more." That can get their attention now, not in the Year 2000.

Senator BENNETT. Another aspect of this, turning it around, Company A works with Bank X. Bank X does send out the list.

Mr. McDaniel, couching it in the very careful terms you describe, Company B works with Bank Y. Bank Y, Mr. Jinnett, follows the more conservative thing and doesn't tell them anything, or just says, come talk to us. Midnight comes. Company A does just fine, survives. Company B has major problems. Does Company B sue its bank for not warning it the way Company A's bank warned it? You have an opportunity, I think, for class action suits on the other hand. If only my bank had met some kind of industry standard of warning, I wouldn't be in the problem I'm in. It's always the class action lawyer's plea that it's somebody else's fault.

Mr. JINNETT. Mr. Chairman, Bank B is relying on actual testing. So rather than giving a list of 15 things to do, they are saying, let's test our systems together. They are relying on the actual testing, rather than just letters.

Senator BENNETT. I see. OK. The question is should the banks be encouraged or, in any way, with Federal power, compelled to notify their customers along the awareness issue that Mr. Miller has described? How far should the Government go to see that banks and insurance companies do reach down the distribution chain and take action that would cause their customers to get involved?

I know that's the question we ultimately have to answer, but any counsel and advice you could give us would be much appreciated.

Mr. McDANIEL. I would still maintain that special legislation mandating that isn't necessary and may well be inappropriate.

Again, the bank's relationship with its customer, which I think is the focus here, is a contractual one. The bank is not Big Brother to their customers and the customers have their own obligations to bring their systems into compliance. The bank's concern is, and should be, the interface with those, especially their key customers, and I think competition is going to drive that. The bank's own self-interest in preserving the integrity of its system will motivate that step being taken.

The bigger concern, and tangential to your question, that I have discussed with our bank clients, the prospect of loan defaults triggered by customers who, because of Year 2000 problems, are significantly adversely affected and become no longer viable or unable to keep the loans current.

Senator BENNETT. Yes.

Mr. McDANIEL. They are struggling with what to do in that situation, especially with respect to older loan documents which are not up for renewal and don't expressly provide for the right to demand such assurances.

So those are real issues, and banks are struggling with them. The question is, is it appropriate that banks handle them in a specific way? My suggestion is simply that, because these issues are so different in so many different contexts, that kind of legislation at least shouldn't be enacted without real deep study.

Senator BENNETT. Yes. As I said in my opening statement, it may not have to be legislation. This could become a safety and soundness issue, where the Federal regulator says, wait a minute, Bank X, you are not doing enough with your customers. We will not mandate the specifics of what you should do, but our examiner comes back and says, you are really quite exposed to loan defaults and other viruses, et cetera, coming through the system because you have not made an attempt, Mr. Jinnett, to deal with your customers or test or warn or send out 15 suggestions or anything. We are going to find that as a safety and soundness issue on your examination.

I do not think the regulators are thinking in those terms right now. They are thinking entirely in terms of the bank's own system, but not in terms of the bank's responsibility or response to competitive pressures to deal with their own customers.

It may well be that all we do from this Subcommittee is call on the regulators to use their power on a safety and soundness examination and that we pass no legislation. The Federal Government does have levers other than the legislative level.

Mr. MILLER. I would concur with what you are saying, Mr. Chairman. For example, I've talked to some major insurance companies and asked them why they haven't been more aggressive at policy renewal times in asking their customers what they are doing on Year 2000. The answer is, "We're doing a lot internally to solve our own programs, but the property and casualty market is real soft right now. So when our sales people are out there, they're not out there to try to antagonize the potential customer. They're out there to sign the deal."

By saying to the customer, "By the way, we want a special premium because you haven't done enough on the Year 2000," that's not how you close the deal. Therefore, they are reluctant to do so.

Right now, what I'm hearing from the insurance companies is the market forces are running the other way. There is no incentive in the short-term because they are trying to sell as much property and casualty insurance as possible. They are not in the face of the customer saying, "Before we renew your policy, give us your Year 2000 plan. Let us look at it and make sure it makes sense."

I also don't know what the forces are in the banking industry right now that would compel them.

I'm with Mr. McDaniel. I'm always reluctant to see new Federal legislation. But I think your idea of asking the regulators to take a long, hard look at creating some kind of incentive system or maybe a regulatory environment that would push the banks much more aggressively, particularly with small- and medium-customers to really come clean as to whether they're doing enough on Year 2000, is a great idea.

Dr. Johnson said, "Nothing like a hanging in the morning to concentrate the mind." The problem is there is no hanging in the morning for a lot of these companies. They think, for 2 or 3 years, they don't have to worry. If they are told their line of credit is going to get pulled or their insurance isn't going to get renewed, then that's a hanging in the morning. That will concentrate their minds.

Senator BENNETT. Yes.

Mr. JINNETT. Mr. Chairman.

Senator BENNETT. Yes?

Mr. JINNETT. I think one thing that technical experts recognize is that testing is maybe 40 to 60 percent of the entire effort in terms of becoming Year 2000 compliant. And with the financial services industry, it's a very interconnected industry. So even if one institution by itself becomes compliant, it may fail because it is networked with somebody who is not.

The only way we're going to know, or the only way the regulators and Congress is going to know that the banking industry, that the financial services industry, as an industry, is compliant, is going to work, not have serious disruption, is to have a sharing of information and some type of industry-wide testing. The financial institutions are nervous about sharing information——

Senator BENNETT. That's right.

Mr. JINNETT. —opening up their files if they are going to be subject to punitive damage suits. The only way you can protect them from punitive damages in this instance is through legislation. In order to encourage industry-wide testing, to get everybody to cooperate with each other and share information, share remediation techniques, they are going to have to be protected from punitive damages, at least.

Senator BENNETT. Senator Grams.

Senator GRAMS. No questions. Thank you, Mr. Chairman.

Senator BENNETT. All right. I have a few more.

Mr. Miller, I was very impressed with your certification process. I understand that some insurance companies charge hundreds of thousands of dollars just to review a company to see if it qualifies for insurance, and part of that review is the Year 2000 compliant thing. First, are you aware of the fact that some insurance companies are doing this? And second, if you are aware of the practice, is your certification process as stringent as theirs?

Mr. MILLER. The answer to the first part of your question, Mr. Chairman, is I have heard that some insurance companies do have a review process. I haven't heard hundreds of thousands, but I have heard $50,000 to $100,000 to do one of these reviews before they will provide insurance for Year 2000.

Is ours as stringent? At the end of the day, I think ours is exceptionally stringent. But I haven't actually seen what the specific review process is that these insurance companies are using for the $50,000 to $100,000.

We are actually talking to an insurance company right now that has asked us to consider whether we would be willing to do this for them. We are just beginning to learn about what they think is adequate. I probably could answer your question a lot better in a few months after I have had this review.

Senator BENNETT. If you could, we would appreciate your sending us that information.

Mr. MILLER. Certainly.

Mr. JINNETT. Mr. Chairman.

Senator BENNETT. Yes?

Mr. JINNETT. I am President of the 2000 Secure Audit Company, which is the audit company for J&H Marsh and McLennan insurance product, 2000 Secure, and we do on-site audits of prospective insureds. It can go into six-figures. It is a very extensive audit. It is not just answering questionnaires. It is actually creating dependency models of an entire company's computer systems and mapping out technical, business, and legal risk. It is very, very extensive and it's ongoing. It involves quarterly monitoring between now and the Year 2000 as well.

So, I am very familiar with the ITAA certification process, and the process that we use for the J&H Marsh and McLennan process is much, much more extensive.

Senator BENNETT. I see. Thank you.

Are insurance companies dropping Year 2000 liability as they renew policies? Does anyone know that?

Mr. JINNETT. Some reinsurance companies in their reinsurance treaties are putting in exclusions for Year 2000 liability. They are putting pressure on the primary insurers.

In the directors and officers liability market, it is a soft market. The primary insurance companies are loathe to put in a Year 2000 exclusion in their primary insurance policies. They are, however, sending out questionnaires, some of them quite detailed, in order to determine if some of the insureds pose bad risks. In those instances, they may fail to renew the D&O policy, they may change the terms or they may take some other action to reduce the risk in the portfolio.

With respect to the business interruption policies, many underwriters have taken the position that they are not meant to cover fortuitous events and therefore, they are sending out awareness letters to bring to the insured's attention that there is a Year 2000 problem, they should deal with it, to reinforce the fact that this is not a fortuitous event. It's not something that's going to catch the insured unawares. They have been notified of it.

Insurers are taking a numbers of steps to identify the risks within each of their lines of business, to decide whether they want to rewrite some of the policy language. If it is an admitted product, they will need the regulator's approval. If it is a surplus lines product, they can do it on their own. The beginning action that we are seeing is at the reinsurance level. It will most likely start to move down to the primary insurance level within the next year.

Mr. MILLER. Just to clarify, Mr. Chairman. I believe that the insurance program that Mr. Jinnett is involved with is when an insurance company offers a specific Year 2000 policy, they do this kind of review. It is not a standard business type of review.

Senator BENNETT. I see.

Mr. MILLER. We are only talking about situations where Marsh and McLennan, and I think there may be one or two others, have specific Year 2000 policies that they are offering. Then they go into this very extensive review. But for the average renewal of a property and casualty line, there's no such review.

Mr. JINNETT. Yes. I should make that clear, that the J&H Marsh and McLennan product is called 2000 Secure. It's to insure against business interruption losses due to Year 2000, provide D&O insurance, provide third-party liability insurance arising out of the Year 2000, and also hot-site expense. It is solely for a Year 2000 event.

Mr. MILLER. I think the number of policies written is so low, and maybe Mr. Jinnett can correct me if I'm wrong, you can count them on a couple of hands. This is not yet a widespread program, neither the Marsh and McLennan, nor the others.

Mr. JINNETT. Yes. There are essentially three policies that are being offered now—the AIG finite risk policy and two risk-transfer policies, J&H Marsh and McLennan's and AON's. They are all in their beginning stages. They are just starting to pick up steam.

Senator BENNETT. OK. Thank you very much.

Mr. MILLER. Could I add one piece of data?

Senator BENNETT. Yes.

Mr. MILLER. I received some data yesterday from Dr. Howard Rubin, who is the Chairman of the Computer Science Department at Hunter College. Dr. Rubin does semiannual surveys and the data I received is from August. He indicated that 6 out of 10 companies have not yet done a complete assessment of the Year 2000 challenge, and only 1 out of 6 have a complete plan in place.

Because you are monitoring Year 2000 on an ongoing basis, Mr. Chairman, I thought that Dr. Rubin's most current data would continue to give you another sleepless night or two. It shows that we are still not making the kind of progress that we hoped.

Mr. JINNETT. Could I add one thing, Mr. Chairman?

Dr. Kappelman, who heads the SIM working group, surveyed companies about a year ago and they had completed maybe 5 percent of their projects. They just resurveyed those same companies and they now have 11 percent of their projects completed.

Dealing with statistics is dangerous. If you put a statistician's one foot on burning coals and the other foot in a pot of freezing cold water, the statistician will say, on average, his feet feel fine. So statistics are dangerous. But taking the statistical analysis, he would say that if they continue at this pace, they are not going to complete their projects until the year 2012, approximately. It is worrisome.

Senator BENNETT. Yes. Well, I will dismiss this panel with this one anecdote, which may be the first recorded Year 2000 meltdown.

Someone in Utah took a name-brand calculator watch and advanced the time date to 11:59 p.m., December 31, 1999, just to see what would happen. One minute later, midnight came, the display went black. He tried resetting the watch to the current date and time and the display was still blank. He then put in a new battery. Blank. So, he took the watch to a repair facility for a diagnosis. He was told that one of the gates in the chip had frozen in the open position and the short-circuit drained the battery and fried the chip. The watch was useless.

That may be the first example, but it demonstrates what we are dealing with. I would think there may be some consumers that would want to file a class action lawsuit if they had bought that kind of watch.

[Laughter.]

Thank you very much.

Mr. JINNETT. Thank you, Mr. Chairman.

Mr. MILLER. Thank you.

Mr. MCDANIEL. Thank you.

Senator BENNETT. We appreciate your testimony. It has been very helpful.

Our next witness is Brian Lane. Mr. Lane is the Director of the Division of Corporate Finance at the SEC. He will discuss the SEC's policy on Year 2000 disclosure. Mr. Lane, we welcome you.

OPENING STATEMENT OF BRIAN J. LANE
DIRECTOR, DIVISION OF CORPORATION FINANCE
U.S. SECURITIES AND EXCHANGE COMMISSION

Mr. LANE. Thank you, Mr. Chairman.

Mr. Chairman and Members of the Subcommittee, I appreciate the opportunity to testify on behalf of the Securities and Exchange Commission regarding the obligation of each public company to disclose the impact of the Year 2000 on their company.

In the interest of time, I am not going to repeat any of my written testimony. Instead, I would like to tell you that the Commission shares your concern about the issue and is taking concrete steps to assure appropriate disclosure by public companies.

As my written testimony explains, under our current rules, the public companies are required to disclose the impact of Year 2000 problem if it is material to their business. If it is not of sufficient consequence to a particular company, the company may, but is not required to, make disclosure. Investment companies and investment advisors have similar requirements.

Rather than draft a rule to compel disclosure when an issue is not material to a company, we prefer to take alternative steps. I think we can be true to our goal of streamlining disclosure and reducing layers of regulation while protecting investors by taking the following three actions.

First, increase awareness of the problem and the disclosure requirement by: A, pointing to our recently issued staff legal bulletin no. 5, which you made reference to in your opening remarks, which addresses Year 2000 disclosure requirements and is available on the Commission's Web site. B, intensifying our efforts with groups such as the American Bar Association, the American Society of Corporate Secretaries, Business Roundtable, small business groups such as the American Business Conference and the Association of Publicly Traded Companies, as well as the Investment Company Institute. C, issuing regular reminders at conferences at which we are speakers. And D, devoting a page on the Commission's Web site to useful information on the Year 2000 issue.

The second action that we are prepared to take is to monitor disclosure of the Year 2000 issues. In the upcoming months, we intend to issue comments with each filing reviewed by my division to direct attention to the staff legal bulletin and ask each issuer to confirm to the staff that there are not any material issues regarding Year 2000 that need to be disclosed.

Additionally, we plan to conduct a focused review of annual disclosures in the upcoming Forms 10–K. The focus will be upon those industries we feel may be most susceptible to Year 2000 problems.

The Division of Investment Management will review all mutual fund prospectuses for Year 2000 disclosure.

The third action is that we want to highlight the fact that this is not just a securities law issue, but a critical investor relations issue as well.

We will be working with the National Investor Relations Institute about encouraging companies, even when they are not required to make disclosure, to address the impact of Year 2000 in their communications with their shareholders. This could be accomplished in a statement in their annual report, perhaps a president's letter to shareholders, or perhaps on a company's Web site. It would not have to be in a document where liability concerns could force lawyers to draft meaningless boilerplate.

Let me conclude my remarks with one observation. Companies have every incentive to provide this disclosure to investors. When material, the Commission rules require it. Separately, analysts and the market may demand it. Good investor relations suggest it. And fear of being wrong compels it. To mandate more may disturb the delicate regulatory balance we strike in determining whether to impose new disclosure requirements on companies.

I would be happy to answer any questions you might have.

Senator BENNETT. Thank you very much.

Why have so few companies done any disclosure with respect to their Year 2000 problem, given the concluding statement?

Mr. LANE. I think part of it is the first action about awareness.

Let me start with the mutual fund companies, which are not in my particular division, but I am familiar with their situation. In the mutual fund industry, most of the Year 2000 concerns are in the administrative area. It should be noted that only 5 of the very largest mutual fund complexes do their own administrative work. The rest of the mutual funds contract out to other transfer agents.

It is primarily just three transfer agents that do all of the recordkeeping and the administrative functions for the investment companies. The biggest one by far is already Year 2000 compliant. They recognized this problem years ago and took steps to correct it. The other two are very close, we are told, and they are being closely monitored. So in the investment company area, the mutual fund area, we think that could be a very good reason why many investment companies are not making disclosure at this time, because it is not material to them.

We have also been working closely with the Investment Company Institute and those five mutual fund families, very large ones, to make sure that they do understand the issue and that they are taking steps to correct it.

Now let me talk about my area, the public companies, which we don't regulate as closely as we regulate broker-dealers and investment advisors.

Clearly, in the broker-dealer area, investment advisors, mutual funds, people that we regulate, we are on top of the issue working very closely with them and monitoring their progress. We will, both in our reports to you and in the upcoming testimony that we will have, talk to you about the progress, not only what we are doing internally at the SEC, but also the industries.

In the area of the public companies, it's a mixed bag, the reason why we aren't getting that much disclosure.

We are getting disclosure and my impression is that disclosure is getting more common in this area. We issued the staff legal bulletin that we referenced, to increase the awareness that the rules do require a focus on any known uncertainty that a company faces. That is the purpose of the management's discussion and analysis requirement that is referred to in my written testimony. We think that the staff legal bulletin, plus the steps that we are taking, will increase the awareness on it.

I think that many companies are already aware, but I pulled a number of 10–K's yesterday and looked at them in preparation of coming here. I pulled some 10–Q's that have been recently filed and took a look at them.

Your opening statement indicated that very few have actually gone the extra step to quantify what their Year 2000 liabilities are. In just the sampling that I pulled and it is not scientific in any sense, I found 10 companies that gave specific dollar amounts that they anticipated. And I am prepared to tell you who they are if you are interested.

There are many other disclosures that vary. Some companies are just saying, we are aware of the Year 2000 problem. We are looking into it. Other companies are saying, we think this could be a problem. We are in the process of examining how it is going to affect the company. Some even go further to say whether they think it will have a material effect on their company. But it is true, it is a growing phenomenon.

Senator BENNETT. Well, let me share with you our experience, and I will mask the name of the company for obvious reasons.

We did the same thing, pulled some 10–K's and found some companies that had reported and had quantified, we called them up and invited them to come to this hearing. You can be a hero. You can be the shining example. This will be wonderful.

The reaction on the part of the CFO with whom my staff spoke was sheer terror at the idea of having any real focus on what they were doing. He said, yes, we put a number, but I guarantee you the number is nowhere near big enough. The more we get into this, the more we realize—and if I am forced to say in a Congressional hearing what the number really is, the competitive disadvantage will be significant. Everybody will be out dumping our stock if they know the size of the number. No way are we going to show up and be subjected to questioning as to where the number that we put out come from, how adequate is it, and what have we found out?

His reaction was, no, we don't want to be the poster child. We don't want to have everybody look at us as the example. We are very nervous about what's eventually going to have to happen.

Obviously, we didn't call them. But the thought occurs to me, if there were tougher disclosure requirements coming from the SEC, that would remove the competitive issue because he could now say, not only do I have to disclose how much this is going to cost my company, but also every other company in our industry is going to have to disclose the same thing, and we won't stand out like a sore thumb. We won't have to worry about the impact on our share price vis-à-vis other competitors' share prices because we will all then have the same hit, and maybe we can convince the market that it's a one-time thing and it doesn't really represent a deterioration of our operating earnings and our stock price won't get hurt. But if we stand out as the only one, our stock price will get hit and everybody else will get by.

Would you comment on that real-life experience?

Mr. LANE. Sure. From the first part of your statement, I really have a two-part response, both for this individual anecdote. If this person indicated to you that the liabilities were far in excess of what they had disclosed, then this company has other problems than just being embarrassed about coming here today.

Senator BENNETT. Sure. But those are developing. See, he still can't quantify it. He can explain his position by saying, when we put the first number in, we had every indication that it was adequate. Now at some point, you are right, he is going to have to come forward with a second number.

Mr. LANE. Exactly. That's the beauty of the disclosure requirement. It is sort of an evergreen. As soon as you know that the circumstances have changed, then you have to modify your disclosure accordingly.

The second part of your question to me really is, well, wouldn't a tougher SEC disclosure rule get better disclosure and protect companies like this that are afraid to make disclosure because they will be put at a competitive disadvantage?

My answer to you would be, no, we don't need a tougher rule. We have the rule now. What the problem is, if there is a problem, and there appears to be a problem in the sense that we aren't getting as many disclosures as we would expect, is that there is concern that companies may not understand that this is another issue that is impacted by the Federal securities laws and that it is required to be disclosed.

I am here to tell you today that it is required. We would tell anybody who called us, it is required. We say at conferences it is required. We put out the staff legal bulletin, and there is every hope that when they realize we are doing the special monitoring——

That is why I have come here today to tell you that we are going to test this, the theory about why people aren't making disclosure. Is it because they have made a determination that it is not material? Or is it because they aren't fully aware of the consequences of this and potentially, to their shareholders?

We will get to the bottom of it, and we will, through the review process, because they have to come across our desks. We will be responding to them directly on this and having them tell us, why is there no disclosure? If they tell us, it is because we made a determination that it is not material, that's OK, then it is consistent with the rule.

Senator BENNETT. Yes. That may well be that this process you have just described constitutes the tougher activity that I was referring to——

Mr. LANE. Without rulemaking, that's right.

Senator BENNETT. —without additional rulemaking.

Mr. LANE. That's right.

Senator BENNETT. Have you seen any company make a disclosure about potential liability? Or is the disclosure tied entirely to the cost of fixing their own system?

Mr. LANE. The ones that I have seen that have actually quantified the numbers have all been the costs that they are incurring, or expect to incur to remediate the problem.

Some disclosure has been good, plain English kind of disclosure about what is the Year 2000 problem. They have gone into a pretty good effort to explain what the ramifications of going to zero might mean on their systems and have suggested that they might also cause problems with some of their vendors or customers and that there may be liability issues. But I would say that's probably the exception rather than the rule.

Senator BENNETT. We started out the hearing talking about the estimates of the liability running as high as $1 trillion. That seems to make it material in just about any industry. I think, frankly, that is bigger than the cost of fixing the system.

Up and down the distribution chain, the various contractual relationships have to be sorted out, as the first panel outlined. I would hope you would spend some time in your effort to increase awareness to make sure they understand that the exposure has to do with liability, as well as the cost of fixing the system.

Senator Grams, do you have anything?

Senator GRAMS. No, Mr. Chairman, I have no questions.

Senator BENNETT. I want to know how many companies are on the road toward completion. You have indicated, not enough. Obviously, you would agree that shareholders have a right to know where their companies are.

Mr. LANE. Absolutely, where it's material to the company.

As you indicated, the magnitude of the economy, as your opening statement detailed, is very significant and it can have very material impacts on the companies themselves.

We think the companies are in the best position to judge for themselves. As you have done as a director yourself, we think that they have to look at it from a liability issue. They have to look at it because we require it, and we like to think that when we speak about what we are looking for and what we are hammering on, that the companies will listen very carefully and respond to that.

The third part of it is, and as you can appreciate as a director of a company, this is an important investor relations issue which I mentioned, and it goes back to your point of don't shareholders need to know this sort of thing?

If shareholders, by reading the paper, by hearing what's going on in Congress, by better understanding what the Year 2000 problem is all about, if they are getting uncomfortable about where their company is vis-à-vis the Year 2000 problem, then the company's got to be thinking, even if it's not material to their company, even if it's not required in the Federal securities laws, that maybe they need to come out with something to comfort the shareholders or respond to analysts, or put something on their Web site that would respond to those concerns. And I think that will happen.

Senator BENNETT. You are not in a position to do anything about this, but I will make the comment, anyway, in the hope that somebody will listen. Again, back to the company where I serve as a director. We had a computer problem about a year ago. It was not caused by the Year 2000. It was caused by a switch-over from a prior system to what was supposed to be bigger and better. It was a disaster. We had customers who would order one item and get 15 or 20. We had other customers who would get nothing.

I was the CEO of that company before I came to Congress and prided myself on leaving the legacy of superb customer service. We were benchmarked by some of the biggest names in the country as they would come out and see how we did customer service. In a matter of 2 to 3 weeks, we destroyed that reputation because the computer software didn't function the way it was supposed to. I think it probably cost us 3 or 4 cents in earnings per share in terms of consumer reaction, and who knows what it cost us in terms of momentum. That's material.

Even though if you look at it in terms of what did you pay in working overtime to get the orders out and handling them manually because the computer wasn't working, well, OK, we can put a dollar cost on that. As I say, I think it was probably 2 or 3 cents per share, which, in terms of market capitalization, ended up in millions and millions of dollars, as the share prices fell, as we didn't meet our numbers and all, you know, how the whole thing works out.

So, I hope businesses will recognize that when they are making this disclosure of the size of their exposure, that it is not just based on, well, it will cost us $2 per line of code to get this fixed and we will do a quick multiple and then we will figure out how much that is. Then we say, well, that's nonmaterial. It can be very material in terms of the impact on the business and the exposure to class action suits and other liability.

Thank you, Mr. Lane. We appreciate your coming here.

Mr. LANE. Thank you.

Senator BENNETT. Our final witness is Robert Austrian. Mr. Austrian is the Senior Enterprise Software Analyst at NationsBanc Montgomery Securities in San Francisco. Also, Mr. Austrian is the author, along with a colleague, Tom Pagel, of the report entitled,

"Millennium Morass—A New Perspective for Every Investor and Business Leader."

We understand, sir, that you will address the disclosure issues from the investor's perspective. We welcome you.

OPENING STATEMENT OF ROBERT B. AUSTRIAN
VICE PRESIDENT & SENIOR ENTERPRISE SOFTWARE ANALYST
NATIONSBANC MONTGOMERY SECURITIES, INC.

Mr. AUSTRIAN. Thank you very much, Mr. Chairman and Members of the Subcommittee. It is, indeed, a pleasure to be invited to share some of our thoughts and to submit some of our existing written materials on this subject and some of the adjacent subject matters that we cover.

I would like to first make mention of my background, that you may understand better the perspective from which I come to bring you my thoughts today. And as well say that I am, in the interest of time, not going to review the entirety of my written submission, but do, in fact, suggest that it contains a great variety of thoughts that I hope you and other Members of the Subcommittee get to address in time.

I have been a securities analyst, really a professional student of technology and of the software industry in particular, first as a participant in that industry, and now as a financial analyst, reviewing that industry for approximately 12 years, and the full duration of my professional career. I am not a lawyer. I am a former industry participant and a financial analyst.

Today, I would like to share some thoughts with you about my view of the nature of the risk in this issue, the acceptability, or the lack thereof, of public disclosure by public companies, which I am responsible for following. Let me leave my opening remarks at that.

As far as the conclusion, which I would like to provide up front, I think, very clearly, that our conclusion is that the level of disclosure from public companies to the investment community is not sufficient at this time.

We ourselves, in the course of the last year, have done a great deal of homework on this subject of the Year 2000 and its risks, its nature, and how it is being addressed. In the course of doing our homework, we sought to assess the readiness of many public companies.

Our own difficulty in assessing the current status of the industry I think is very telling and indicates that, through existing public filings, interviews with managements, and our own survey sent to 5,000 people, which was returned by less than 2 percent, that the amount of information is really not adequate.

I would also like to point out that our conclusion is that the risk in this area is both greater, faster changing, and happening more quickly than is generally believed.

Very importantly, while most have focused on the risk and the liability in terms of dollars that may need to be spent, few have adequately addressed the issues of the shortage of time and labor, both of which in our report, and in our opinion, are the key factors, not simply monetary considerations, as the key risk.

Today, there are approximately, if not exactly, 800 days, if my math was correct, until the beginning of the new millennium. I would like to also point out in that vein that January 1st of the Year 2000 is in no way the commencement of the problem. You pointed out with your watch example that systems are already beginning to fail and there is no magic day, that first day, that represents the beginning of our discovery about what the real outcome of this problem is.

So just as attention is over-acutely focused on dollars and not sufficiently focused on time and labor, the deadline as well is a bit misrepresented if it is generally believed to be January 1st of the Year 2000.

A special consideration of this subject, I believe, is the intertwined nature of systems, which many of the panelists and you yourself had referred to earlier. This problem, in the software and systems, the embedded chips of all kinds, really is much broader than lives within the sides of the walls of any single business and the financial community was specifically mentioned where we have firsthand knowledge of how that is so. But in other areas, the intertwined nature of the systems is, indeed, a key and a risk that should be addressed very carefully.

Mostly, I confess, as I did up front, that I am not a lawyer. So, I would like to spend more time not on the legal aspects, per se, but, rather, on our experience with the disclosure and its adequacy or lack thereof.

We also review filings with the SEC and very, very carefully, literally, with tweezers, if you will, all of the filings from the roughly 50 to 100 companies that are suppliers of software to industries around the world. These are oftentimes the systems which are solutions to the Year 2000 problem, where there is such a packaged solution available.

We too found remarkably few disclosures about this issue over the last year. Indeed, we found that those disclosures which did exist tended simply to put forth a dollar amount if it was viewed to be a material risk, or to state simply that it was material, without a dollar amount or that it was immaterial.

Going back to my point about labor and time being as important as dollars, I would like to point out that flavor of disclosure really is inadequate in terms of helping even professional analysts, no less general investors on the street, understand the nature of businesses' dependency on systems and those systems' weaknesses as relates to the Year 2000.

We do, therefore, believe that much greater levels of disclosure are needed and we will leave it to your Subcommittee, the SEC, and the lawyers to help figure out exactly how to achieve that, or perhaps on a future occasion, we can make some suggestions beyond the few that we will hit today, which are more general in nature. But we do want to provide our conclusion that a very much more practicable and specific category of information and type of information is needed for investors to understand the risks.

I would also like to echo earlier remarks that, despite the lack of disclosure, businesses appear very, very early on in actually addressing their issues and risks in this area.

Assessment, as you know from your work in the subject to date, is simply the earliest step in understanding the size and nature of the problem and it doesn't even specifically include an action plan for how to fix the problem if there is a fix available.

Polls as recently as this August of Fortune 500 class IT directors who run the infrastructure for some of America's finest companies, this survey showed that as few as 16 percent have actually begun implementing a full- fledged strategy, while many more, approximately 24 percent, have some kind of a plan in place.

We have understood through past testimony that it has been suggested that if investors are concerned and have the desire for more information than has been provided, that they should simply ask. Indeed, we are in the business of asking every day.

We asked, through our 5,000 surveys earlier this year, two senior IT managers for information about their progress in this area and what they were doing, if anything. As I said earlier, less than 2 percent, only 67 of the companies responded. And while this was a letter that arrived in the mail that they were unfamiliar with, we had certainly hoped, given who it was coming from and the seriousness of the question, that we would have more satisfactory results. But we did not.

I would like to point out as well that software companies, as opposed to companies in general, businesses in general, may require special disclosure requirements, or at least should be compelled to provide special levels of disclosure.

Only recently have leading companies in this country begun to disclose how much of their business, if any, is really influenced by the demand, the good news coming from the need to address the Year 2000 problem.

The Oracle Corporation, one of the leaders in its 10–K, its year ending in May of this year, I believe, actually indicated that they were concerned looking ahead that demand might abate for their products, since their products have been enjoying extra demand as a result of businesses seeking to fix their problem. This, I believe, is the first such statement by any public company of the roughly 200 that supply answers to this and other software-centric information technology problems.

Likewise, the chief executive of another leading company, People Soft, has only recently begun addressing his opinion that their business may experience a slowdown, although I believe this has so far been simply a verbal indication, not a written one.

We were also asked to put a few thoughts together today concerning which industries might be most exposed.

In this vein, I would like to indicate that all businesses are exposed, either because they themselves and their own systems may be victims of this bug, if you wish to call it that, or because they are interdependent on other businesses and other industries that themselves may have problems. Clearly, financial, insurance, and investment companies and, as well, the manufacturing industry, may be most exposed because of their use of date-intensive calculations in their businesses.

In summary, I would like to leave you with just a few points.

First, I believe, based on what I have read from your Subcommittee and what I have heard today, that you are dead on target, and nothing less, to be looking at this issue in the way you are looking at the issue, and that this is a leading forum for discovery about the nature of the problem and how to solve it.

Second, while I welcome and suggest much greater disclosure by public companies, as we as experts continue to be frustrated with the level of disclosure, that I doubt there's a simple and single answer which will emerge about how to make that happen, although I would enjoy an opportunity to think about that one some more.

Third is that your watch is not the first example at all, and there is a litany of examples going back several years, though they are not very public, about this having become a problem.

Fourth would be that there is a real risk of recession and Economist Yardeni is not the first, although he is one of the more public to make a statement recently about the risk of some kind of slowdown in our industry.

And I remind you that technology is pushing 15 percent of the Standard & Poor's 500 and is growing to be one of the most dominant market cap sectors of the S&P, itself is likely to have some kind of a slowdown.

So, overall, industry could certainly experience a taste of that.

Fifth, and last is to reiterate that we do find that labor and time are major risks and that attention should be focused not simply on dollars spent. That figure that one company might offer up is not adequate to understand the nature of their burden and whether they are addressing it in a timely and sophisticated manner.

Mr. Chairman, I thank you very much for your time and would welcome any questions, and hope that if I don't answer them today, that they may be contained in our report which we have submitted for the record.

Senator BENNETT. Thank you. We appreciate your being here and your comments.

I didn't understand fully about what you were saying about the demand side, especially with Oracle. Is the CEO of Oracle saying that there's going to be less demand for his products because they are not 2000 compliant? Or is he saying—is that where we are?

Mr. AUSTRIAN. Let me clarify the point.

Senator BENNETT. Yes.

Mr. AUSTRIAN. Software companies that provide solutions, those solutions that are compliant with the Year 2000, have been, in our opinion, enjoying extra demand these past years, as the forward-looking customers of theirs have sought to address their problem, whether they were looking to switch, as your former business did switch from one system to another, for some reason, or because they need to enhance their existing system.

Businesses that supply solutions, such as Oracle and PeopleSoft, who are just two examples—there happen to be larger ones—are now saying they believe that as we get closer to, into and beyond the Year 2000, since they will have satisfied much pent-up demand from customers upgrading earlier this year and last year, that they may experience some kind of slowdown at that time.

Senator BENNETT. I see. But not currently.

Mr. AUSTRIAN. Well, the language as written is a little bit unclear as to when the beginning and end points are. Our professional investment advice to our investment customers is that we are now probably approaching the end of a period of extra demand for solutions from these companies, from customers who have been forward-looking and who have been replacing their problem systems over the last several years.

Mind you that the solutions that we are talking about which cost many millions of dollars, generally, if not tens of millions, take time to put in place. They take time to be tested and to become functional. So working back from the Year 2000, you can understand why demand for these products might be added to in 1994, 1995, 1996, and 1997, and begin to abate later on.

Senator BENNETT. That is counterintuitive to me. I am not following you and that is why I raised the issue. Are you saying that the off-the-shelf products, presumably available from Oracle and PeopleSoft, are beginning to see a flattening of demand?

Mr. AUSTRIAN. That is correct. That is what I was saying.

Senator BENNETT. But does that mean that in terms of the overall Year 2000 problem, that the rest of the problem has got to come from in-house fixing, because if you just talk about off-the-shelf products, then if the demand is slackening, that means the problem is being solved. And I don't think the problem is being solved.

Mr. AUSTRIAN. I agree that the problem is not fully being solved. However, off-the-shelf solutions are only viable as replacements up to some point in time, at which there is no longer sufficient time for them to be employed as a replacement.

Senator BENNETT. I see. Now, I'm with you.

Mr. AUSTRIAN. I apologize for the confusion.

Senator BENNETT. No, no. It took me a little while to catch on.

Mr. AUSTRIAN. I will point out that this concept, really, of some specific timing of when these kinds of demand events unfold, is relatively new in the financial sector and particularly in the areas of the software community, where, through 1997, I would say we have seen the first instances of attention with some specificity to the timing to these issues.

Senator BENNETT. Well, the issue you raise with respect to time and talent goes to the question of testing.

I have been interested in having the reaction of people who are not as familiar with the issue as maybe they should be, which is, oh, Bill Gates is going to figure something out and we will all buy it from him and the problem will go away. It's a relatively simple fix. And I have said, no. Even if such a fix were available, you have to have the time to put it in place and then test it, because you don't know where the code is lurking that will—back to the watch analogy—fry that particular chip. You have to run the new system and see what the problems are and then run it again after you think you have fixed the problem and discover that there are other problems, and so on.

In our earlier hearing, talking about the banking industry, one of the witnesses said that if a bank or major financial institution does not have his problem solved by September 1998, it is too late. The reason being, for a bank, it has to test the solution. And by September 1998, they have only about a year left of weekends on which to run the test because they can't run the test on the software while they are doing the standard business. They have to do it on the weekends when the bank is otherwise shut down. That is really only about 50 opportunities with holidays and other circumstances and that is not enough.

Mr. AUSTRIAN. There are a great many nuances to the problem. I can only recommend that people in Government and in business responsible in some way for helping find a solution read through the materials available in the market, which there is a growing supply of.

Second, I would reiterate that off-the-shelf software packages are not available for the great majority of systems that exist.

Senator BENNETT. Right.

Mr. AUSTRIAN. Our reports later-focus on the availability of time, which you mentioned, and of labor, which is a considerably constrained pool of labor that's fully employed and not growing.

Senator BENNETT. We dealt with that in one of the previous hearings as well.

Right now, the assumption is that if you go to work on fixing the code in your system, it is going to cost you about $1 per line of code. Given the finite number of people who are capable of doing that, and the timeline of training other people, by the year 1999, it is going to be up to as much as $6 per line of code to get somebody in who can do that. The labor pool is small and, as you say, not growing. That is one of the reasons this number is going up.

Before you leave, could you address the issue with which we opened the hearing, that of liability, and what you see from an investor's point of view in terms of the various liabilities that companies face?

Mr. AUSTRIAN. I will briefly and also I would refer to the written version of our testimony, which includes a little more detail.

We do perceive that there is a very real and large liability risk. But the contracts, literally as written, from suppliers of software, may seek to indemnify those vendors, although I am not certain that would stand up ultimately. I just don't know.

As far as businesses themselves, I think that the liability risk is great by virtue of my understanding of the way in which those companies are so desperately dependent upon their information technology to exist, no less to thrive.

I know in my business experience, as you indicated in your business, that technology interruption does happen and it is extremely painful when it does. When a business has a risk of a total system failure, even for a short time, I don't think there is any question that there is a liability there.

I am not, as I confess, a lawyer, so I don't know literally the ins and outs. I don't know that anybody in the financial industry as a professional analyst is sufficiently up to speed on that, either. However, I do very much believe that there is a real risk inside of businesses from their use of systems, both software and embedded technology.

Senator BENNETT. Let's go to those software companies you are talking about. They are not going to like the analogy I am just about to draw, and I assure them there is no attempt to label them in any fashion. But you know, as does any sophisticated investor, that tobacco companies do not sell for the same PE ratio as other industries because of the liability cloud that hangs over them. That investor does not know that the earnings in the out-years will, in fact, be there because there is always the possibility that a class action suit will make it through the courts and win and the tobacco company will be shut down.

That is one of the reasons why the tobacco companies have entered into this global settlement, because it means that future earnings, even if they are lower, are now going to be there and investors can put PE ratios on those future earnings and thereby see the value of the stock go up, even while the earnings of the company goes down.

Does that hold for software companies who face the possibility of having huge lawsuits brought against them, saying, we in our company had major Year 2000 failures because your software was the one we used? Therefore, we are going to take all of the lawsuits that have been filed against us and pass them on to you and the burden ultimately on a software company of simply defending itself against all those lawsuits, let alone prevailing, becomes so overwhelming, that the company could go under. Is that a calculation, in your investor analysis, of the software industry?

Mr. AUSTRIAN. It is certainly not a calculation that we have performed. I think the reason that I would conclude I needn't perform it on any high-probability basis is, as I understand it, that while the tobacco industry perhaps is accused of some form of systematic gross negligence or some similar understanding that it has had over a long period of time a potential change to its business practices, I don't see any analogous behaviors in the software industry whatsoever.

In general, software companies use their greatest level of cleverness to create software products that accommodate the widest range of potentialities, that is, in fact, what software programmers have to do every day. They spend the great bulk of their time, for example, making their software capable of accommodating the exception cases, not the rules, not the norms, but the exceptions, so that their systems don't fail.

I know that our industry, the software vendor industry, has spent a good measure of effort in trying to make its products as forward-looking, as flexible and accommodating as they possibly can, and certainly not in any way to ever misrepresent their product's functionality.

To that end, the contracts that they sign with customers, be they BankBoston, which certainly is a customer of many of these companies, the few I have mentioned and the many that we follow, or others, simply include language that requires the software to live up to very, very specific capabilities and none further than that, as a matter of the contract.

I don't think that there is any systematic oversight or deceit on the part of the software vendors. Quite the reverse. As I have pointed out, they have enjoyed several years, I think, of excellent demand for their products precisely because they have made them generally compliant with this potentiality, and all the others that face the business leader.

Senator BENNETT. I think Mr. Jinnett in the first panel also gave us some defenses that lawyers for these companies, either software or hardware, would use.

Thank you very much. I appreciate your being here.

In conclusion, as we close this hearing, I want to revisit our last hearing and make a report of where we are so that it will be in the Subcommittee record.

At that time, we had all of the financial regulatory agencies here to discuss their efforts and the efforts of the institutions that they regulate to become Year 2000 compliant—the SEC, the OCC, and others. We asked each regulatory agent to provide us with periodic updates of their progress.

In addition, I sent a request to the General Accounting Office to evaluate the status and the progress of each of these agencies, so that we might have some benchmark with which to gauge their progress.

The GAO has substantially completed its initial assessment of one financial regulatory agency, the National Credit Union Administration. I will include the GAO statement in the hearing record, and remind those other regulatory agencies that the GAO will be visiting them shortly to assist in identifying their status and evaluating their plans for corrective action.

Due to the lack of time and the need to maintain continuity of thought, I will briefly summarize the GAO testimony with respect to NCUA.

The GAO reports that NCUA is not as far along in its assessment of Year 2000 compliance as OMB and the GAO guidelines to Federal agencies recommend that they be. While the NCUA has taken positive steps to address Year 2000 problems, the GAO reports the following:

NCUA does not have an accurate picture of where credit unions and vendors stand in resolving such problems. NCUA lacks a formal contingency plan to address potential Year 2000 problems.

NCUA has not yet ensured that credit union auditors address Year 2000 problems in connection with internal management control audits which guard against error, carelessness, and fraud.

And NCUA lacks qualified staff to conduct examination work in complex systems areas. It is in the process of hiring one auditor and is considering hiring two more. It may well be that is not a sufficient number.

Inasmuch as one in four Americans have membership in over 11,000 credit unions nationwide, this is an important issue for all of us. Federally insured credit union employees are responsible for managing almost $326 billion in assets.

Now, I encourage NCUA to accelerate its Year 2000 activities. I commend the GAO for completing this first study in a significantly appropriate time period. And if there are any out there feeling smug that the NCUA has been singled out, I repeat my earlier comment, that the GAO is coming around to see the rest of the regulatory agencies as well, and that there will be, as there has been with NCUA, a report to this Subcommittee of what the GAO finds.

I thank all of the witnesses. This has been a very useful hearing. This is a problem that requires the kind of attention and expertise that you have brought to the Subcommittee.

The hearing is adjourned.

[Whereupon, at 11:55 a.m., the hearing was adjourned.]

[Prepared statements and additional material supplied for the record follows:]

PREPARED STATEMENT OF SENATOR ROBERT F. BENNETT

In Subcommittee hearings held over the summer, we learned that the Year 2000 problem is more than a computer problem; it is a pervasive business issue for which there is no quick fix. Businesses rely on computer systems for nearly every aspect of their operations—from operating elevators to calculating interest on loans, to launching satellites. A failure in one computer system could not only devastate the operation it controls, but could also domino through other systems and cause other seemingly unrelated operations to shut down. As a result, virtually every business in this country will face a stream of potential direct and contingent liabilities based on the failures of their own systems or those of their business partners.

Estimates of the litigation companies could face as a result of the Year 2000 problem now exceed $1 trillion. Despite this incredible figure, individual companies are not talking about what specific liabilities they face or how they plan to manage their litigation risk. This silence raises two very important questions that we plan to explore in today's hearing.

First, what should individual companies be doing to identity and manage their Year 2000 litigation risks and what can the Federal Government do to help?

If there is, indeed, more than a trillion dollars worth of litigation lurking in the next century, what should individual companies be doing to identity and manage that risk? It seems that few companies have been able to determine whether and to what extent they are vulnerable. Companies that are unable to determine their specific risks will certainly not be able to manage them or properly disclose them to the public.

That leads me to the second, and perhaps more important question. Should individual companies be required by law to disclose the projected expenditure and legal and operational uncertainties associated with their Year 2000 remediation efforts?

I believe that investors have a right to know what type and amount of risk individual companies face as a result of the Year 2000 problem. Nevertheless, a review of 10–K's published on the SEC's EDGAR database reveals that very few companies have made specific disclosures with regard to the Year 2000 problem. Most of the disclosures that have been made state generally that the companies are spending money to fix the problem. Despite the enormous projected litigation figures, companies are not reporting specific exposure.

The SEC recently issued a legal interpretation recommending that companies properly disclose the legal and operational risks and uncertainties related to the Year 2000 problem. While I look forward to the SEC's testimony on how they plan to enforce this interpretation, I question whether a legal interpretation is sufficient to encourage companies to make appropriate disclosures.

I believe that some stronger action, perhaps in the form of a law, is necessary to require, rather than simply encourage, companies to keep investors informed. Such a law could require companies to disclose, on an ongoing basis, the projected expenditures and legal and operational uncertainties associated with their Year 2000 remediation efforts. This type of law would help to ensure that investors and the general public are made aware of the progress of remediation efforts within U.S. companies and the direct and contingent liabilities those companies face as a result of the Year 2000 problem.

Every potential investor has a right to those facts, and the burden must be on the corporation to disclose them. It is unfair and unrealistic to expect an individual investor in a corporation or an individual depositor at a financial institution to make those inquiries and get accurate information on their own.

Today's witnesses will discuss the potential liability companies face as a result of the Year 2000 problem and offer recommendations on what can be done to manage that risk.

In conclusion, and as we close this hearing on Year 2000 liability and disclosure, I want to revisit our last Year 2000 compliance hearing. At that time we had all of the financial regulatory agencies here to discuss their efforts and the efforts of the institutions that they regulate to become Year 2000 compliant. We asked each regulatory agency to provide us with periodic updates on their progress.

In addition, I sent a request to the General Accounting Office (GAO) to evaluate the status and progress of each of these agencies so that we might have some benchmark by which to gauge their progress. The GAO has substantially completed its initial assessment of one financial regulatory agency, the National Credit Union Administration, and I will include this GAO statement in the hearing record and remind those other regulatory agencies, that the GAO will be visiting them shortly to assist them in identifying their status and in evaluating their plans for corrective action.

Due to the lack of time and the need to maintain continuity of thought, I will briefly summarize the GAO testimony. GAO reports that NCUA is not as far along in its assessment of Year 2000 compliance as OMB and GAO guidelines to Federal Agencies recommend. While NCUA has taken positive steps to address the Year 2000 problems, GAO reports that:

- NCUA does not have an accurate picture of where credit unions and vendors stand in resolving such problems.
- NCUA lacks a formal contingency plan to address potential Year 2000 problems.
- NCUA has not yet ensured that credit union auditors address Year 2000 problems in connection with internal management control audits which guard against error, carelessness, and fraud.
- NCUA lacks the qualified staff to conduct examination work in complex systems areas. It is in the process of hiring one EDP auditor and is considering hiring two more.

Inasmuch as one in four Americans have membership in over 11,000 credit unions nationwide, this is an important issue for all of us. Federally insured credit union employees are responsible for managing almost $326 billion in assets. In order to ensure that credit union employees can continue to provide top notch service to their members, we want them to have the best supervisory support and assistance possible. I encourage NCUA to accelerate its Year 2000 activities and I commend the GAO for this, the first in a series of evaluations on Y2K compliance of financial regulatory agencies.

PREPARED STATEMENT OF SENATOR ALFONSE M. D'AMATO

Good morning. First of all, I would like to commend Chairman Bennett for calling this hearing on liability issues originating from the Year 2000 computer problem.

The Year 2000 problem is tremendously complicated because it affects all levels of Government and every private business. The Banking Committee, and this Subcommittee, have worked to focus the attention of the financial industry and its Federal regulators on the need for immediate action. And while business and Government should be working right now to prevent a computer catastrophe in January 2000, the reality is that computer problems will occur, and some of them will be very complicated and very expensive to fix. That brings us to the subject of today's hearing—liability—or who is responsible if things go wrong. Mr. Chairman, I am glad to see that, through this Subcommittee, you are diligently pursuing all aspects of the Year 2000 problem.

Although the focus of this hearing goes beyond banks alone, I must say that I am concerned about the poor progress that many banks have made on the Year 2000 problem. The bank regulators now say that, despite efforts to focus industry attention on this ticking time bomb, many banks still have not taken even the most basic steps to prepare for Year 2000. Most larger banks are hard at work. But smaller banks, especially community banks, are in poor shape. Fifteen percent of these banks have done virtually nothing to address the Year 2000. Another 20 percent are only just waking up to the problem. And they don't have 2 years to do the work: They need to fix their computers within the next year so that they will have enough time for testing.

Mr. Chairman, this is a disaster in the making. Both the Full Committee and, I am sure, this Subcommittee will hold the bank regulators responsible for moving the industry forward on this problem.

Unfortunately, although banking institutions are not where they should be, they are at least ahead of the rest of industry. Experts have estimated that only a fraction—no more than 30 percent—of U.S. companies have seriously looked at their Year 2000 risks.

The other 70 percent will be held accountable, by their customers, business partners, and shareholders. If business is interrupted or computer repair costs are unexpectedly high, or if ruinous litigation results from inattention to the Year 2000 problem, company directors and officers will be held responsible. They cannot claim that they had never heard of the Year 2000 problem, and they certainly cannot claim that the arrival of January 1, 2000 was unexpected.

Even companies that have worked diligently to prepare for 2000 may run into trouble with suppliers or partners who were not so careful. Software or equipment that was designed to work well into the next millennium may break down completely if it receives bad data from outside the company. This raises complicated problems of liability, warranties, and disclosure. I see that our witnesses today are well-qualified to discuss some of these problems.

These issues raise the possibility of a blizzard of litigation, reaching perhaps into the trillions of dollars, starting in the next few years. Should Congress act to address liability issues associated with Year 2000? Is there a need for legislation that would clarify disclosure obligations or protect companies against lawsuits?

I welcome the witnesses who appear before the Subcommittee today, especially Mr. Jinnett who is here from New York. I look forward to hearing your views on these questions.

Mr. Chairman, once again, I thank you for calling this hearing on an extremely important issue.

PREPARED STATEMENT OF SENATOR CHUCK HAGEL

Good morning and welcome to our witnesses.

We are here to examine the enormous potential liability companies face as a result of the Year 2000 computer problem. Industries are already facing substantial costs associated with fixing their computer systems to be Year 2000 compliant. Will the looming date change bring severe financial consequences as a result of litigation? What can Congress do to ensure a smooth transition?

Another area of importance is the issue of investor disclosures. When considering a potential investment, should investors be aware of the costs that will be incurred by these companies? What role should the SEC play in forcing disclosure?

I look forward to hearing from our witnesses.

PREPARED STATEMENT OF JEFF JINNETT
PRESIDENT, LEBOEUF COMPUTING TECHNOLOGIES, L.L.C. AND
OF COUNSEL, LEBOEUF, LAMB, GREENE & MACRAE, L.L.P.

OCTOBER 22, 1997

Summary

POTENTIAL YEAR 2000 LITIGATION—Any prediction as to the ultimate litigation which will result from the Year 2000 computer problem is pure speculation, since little substantial litigation has been reported on the Year 2000 computer problem and we do not know how much necessary corrective work will ultimately not be completed. However, if the Gartner Group prediction is accurate that as many as one-half of the companies with the Year 2000 computer problem will not become fully compliant by January 1, 2000, some Year 2000 litigation appears inevitable.

IDENTIFYING AND REDUCING Y2K RISKS—The first step in a Year 2000 risk management program is recognizing that the Year 2000 computer problem poses not only technical issues and risks, but also business and legal issues and risks. The following are examples of steps a company can take to identify and reduce Y2K business and legal risks.

Dependency Models—Enterprises often create technical dependency models mapping out how the enterprise's products and services depend on internal computer systems (internal dependencies) and can be impacted by the noncompliancy of third parties (external dependencies). These technical dependency models would be of significantly greater utility to an enterprise if expanded to include business and legal information and factors.

Loss Scenario Analysis—After the enterprise's technical staff has prepared a list of possible technical loss scenarios, ranked according to magnitude of impact on the enterprise, the above dependency model could be augmented with business and legal risk factors, so as to assist the enterprise in running simulations to determine the likely business and legal impact of each potential technical failure scenario. Top management could then take preventive steps to eliminate or reduce the possible business/legal risk associated with the technical failures most likely to occur and which have the greatest adverse impact on the enterprise.

Third-Party Litigation Risk—Enterprises should consider the possibility that they may become involved in litigation due to the failures of business partners to become compliant. Plaintiffs' attorneys may not be able at the outset of litigation to determine why a defendant's computer systems suffered a "hard" crash or "soft" crash and will have to assume that third parties which share data or software with the defendant may have contributed to the computer system failure. The plaintiff's attorneys are likely to sue not only the primary defendant, but also any business partner which conceivably could have played a part in the system failure due to the sharing of contaminated data or software.

Creation of Due-Diligence Record—Enterprises should take all necessary steps to create a due-diligence record which could be introduced into evidence in litigation, if necessary, to show that the enterprise acted in good faith, using commercially reasonable efforts to solve its Year 2000 problem. The enterprise should review its Year 2000 corrective plan against currently available industry metrics as to remediation and testing costs and methods in order to confirm that the plan adopted by the enterprise matches the current industry best practices.

Handling the Y2K "Perception Problem"—If a public company's shareholders develop concerns over the company's Y2K status due to "doomsday" articles in the press, the shareholders might "short" the company's stock. The enterprise could consider using Y2K audit reports and the securing of Y2K insurance to reassure shareholders that the enterprise is at low risk of a Year 2000 failure. The company could also create a rapid response team to handle press inquiries if Y2K-based system problems arise.

HOW THE FEDERAL GOVERNMENT CAN HELP THE PRIVATE SECTOR—Congress can be of considerable assistance to the financial services industry in its efforts to solve its Y2K problem and also promote fuller disclosure of Y2K issues and information.

Y2K Litigation "Safe Harbor"—Due to fears of providing plaintiffs' attorneys with litigation "ammunition," financial institutions may be reluctant to engage in industry-wide Y2K information-sharing efforts. This fear of litigation exposure is heightened due to the potential imposition of punitive damages on defendants. In order to encourage financial institutions to become fully compliant and to share necessary information with other institutions, I recommend that this Subcommittee consider introducing legislation to provide a "safe harbor" from punitive damages for the financial institutions which establish that they have made a good faith effort to become Year 2000 compliant and which cooperate with industry-wide sharing of Y2K information as may be requested by appropriate regulatory authorities. The demonstration of a good faith effort to become Year 2000 compliant could be made by a national bank, for example, by passing a Year 2000 compliancy audit conducted by the Office of the Comptroller of the Currency. For financial institutions where no Federal regulatory authority has planned to conduct extensive Y2K audits, a quasi-public entity could be established by Congress to conduct the audits.

Why Punitive Damages Are Inappropriate in the Y2K Situation—Punitive damages are imposed to punish reprehensible conduct and to deter others from similar behavior. This simply does not apply to the Year 2000 computer problem. As Dr. Leon Kappelman has demonstrated, over the past 35 years companies have saved far more in computer memory costs (by using two digits for date fields rather than four digits) than they will spend on Y2K remediation and, therefore, the use of two digits for year date fields constituted good business judgment. Further, since the Y2K problem is a onetime occurrence, imposing punitive damages on an individual defendant in a Y2K litigation will not serve any deterrence function whatsoever, either with respect to the specific defendant or to other potential defendants.

Additional aspects of a Y2K litigation "safe harbor" could be considered, including: (a) the prohibition of liability for noneconomic "pain and suffering" losses; (b) elimination of joint and several liability in favor of a proportionate liability standard; (c) a required determination by the court as to whether the plaintiff's cause of action is frivolous, with the imposition of reasonable attorney's fees and costs if determined to be frivolous; and/or, (d) a requirement that the plaintiff establish proof by "clear and convincing evidence" rather than merely by a "preponderance of the evidence."

CONCLUSION—If financial institutions adopt a comprehensive Y2K *risk management* approach rather than merely a technical remediation approach, they should be better able to identify and reduce their technical, business, and legal Y2K risks. In this effort, open disclosure by financial institutions of Y2K compliancy status to their counterpart financial partners, sharing of remediation techniques and other information sharing would aid in the industry-wide Y2K effort. The financial industry's justifiable concerns over providing plaintiffs' attorneys with ammunition through this disclosure makes it imperative that Congress consider enacting legislation creating a Y2K litigation "safe harbor" shielding financial institutions from excessive litigation risks (such as punitive damages), provided the institutions make a good faith effort to become Year 2000 compliant and participate in industry-wide sharing of Y2K information, as requested by appropriate regulatory authorities.

Introduction

Mr. Chairman and distinguished Members of the Subcommittee, my name is Jeff Jinnett and I am President of LeBoeuf Computing Technologies, L.L.C., a business subsidiary of the law firm of LeBoeuf, Lamb, Greene & MacRae, L.L.P. of which law firm I was formerly a Partner and now serve as Of Counsel. I appreciate the opportunity to again testify before this Subcommittee. I wish to note that the testimony

I give today represents my personal views and does not necessarily represent the views of either LeBoeuf Computing Technologies or its parent law firm. Consistent with the expressed scope of this hearing, my testimony will be devoted to assessing: (a) the potential litigation which may result from the Year 2000 computer problem and its impact on the financial services industry; (b) how businesses in the private sector can use a *risk management* approach rather than merely a technical remediation approach to reduce their potential exposure to the Y2K problem; and, (c) how the Federal Government can assist the financial services industry in its Y2K efforts and promote full disclosure of Y2K issues and information by enacting a Y2K litigation "safe harbor."

Potential Year 2000 Litigation

In testimony before the U.S. House of Representatives, Ann Coffou, Managing Director of the Giga Information Group, predicted that litigation resulting from the Year 2000 computer problem may near or exceed $1 trillion. (*See* Hearings before the U.S. House of Representatives Science Committee et al. on March 20, 1997, at the URL of "http://www.itpolicy.gsa.gov/mks/yr2000/hearing.htm.") If this occurs, Year 2000 litigation costs would exceed by many times the estimated $300 billion total annual direct and indirect cost of all civil litigation in the United States. (*See* Jack Kemp, "Common Good Above Profits," *The National Law Journal*, Nov. 4, 1996, at A20; H. Moskowitz & R. Wallace, "Loser Pays: A Deterrent to Frivolous Claims," *The New York Law Journal*, March 7, 1996, at p. 2; Robert Smith, "Saving Ourselves from Being Lawyered to Death," *The Washington Post*, December 23, 1996, at C04.)

Why Litigation is Probably Inevitable

Of course, any prediction as to the ultimate litigation which will result from the Year 2000 computer problem is pure speculation, since little substantial litigation has been reported on the Year 2000 computer problem and we do not know how much necessary corrective work will ultimately not be completed. However, if the Gartner Group prediction is accurate that as many as one-half of the companies with the Year 2000 computer problem will not become fully compliant by January 1, 2000, some Year 2000 litigation appears inevitable. (*See e.g.*, Gartner Group, "Year 2000 Problem Gains National Attention" at the URL of "http://www.com links.com/mag/accr.htm.")

The reasons for this high failure rate are varied: (a) too many companies are starting too late; (b) the companies are not devoting sufficient personnel and funds to the corrective effort; (c) there are not enough trained software programmers available, in any event, to fix all of the software code requiring correction; (d) not enough time and resources will be devoted to the testing phase, which could be the most expensive and time-consuming phase for many companies; (e) even if a particular company becomes fully compliant, its systems may become contaminated by data or software supplied by outside third parties who have not become compliant; and, (f) the city or geographic area in which the company has its offices may not have compliant telecommunications or electric utility systems, resulting in infrastructure failures.

Cascade Effect of Litigation

The failure of a large percentage of companies in the financial services sector could have a cascading effect. First will come business dislocations due to breached contracts, delivery of defective products and services, accidents resulting in personal injuries and property damage and business interruptions. These events may cause the stock prices of public companies to drop, leading to shareholder derivative suits against the boards of directors alleging securities fraud based on inadequate disclosure of Year 2000 problems, waste of corporate assets and breach of fiduciary duty. Affected companies may then sue the vendors of the hardware and software responsible for the computer system failures, as well as computer consultants to the company responsible for overall system design. Many of the entities sued will attempt to recover litigation defense costs and other damages from their insurance carriers, leading to coverage disputes.

Although most of the potential Year 2000 litigation is likely to commence after January 1, 2000, some of the litigation will be filed prior to that date due to concerns of plaintiffs' counsel that claims may be subject to applicable State statutes of limitation dating, for example, from the date of original delivery and acceptance of an allegedly noncompliant item of hardware or software. Rather than explore in detail here the complex issues of relevant causes of action available to plaintiffs and possible defenses available to defendants, I have appended for the Subcommittee's review an article I authored entitled "The Millennium Bug Strikes Back" which appeared in the June 1997 issue of *The Los Angeles Lawyer* magazine which analyzes these issues in-depth. Instead, the following section will examine steps which companies in the financial services industry might consider taking in order to attempt to identify and reduce business and legal risks which they face due to the Year 2000 computer problem.

Identifying and Reducing Y2K Risks

The first step in a Year 2000 risk management program is recognizing that the Year 2000 computer problem poses not only technical issues and risks, but also business and legal issues and risks. A technical Year 2000 plan is usually comprised of four stages or phases: (a) inventory of computer systems affected by the Y2K problem (hardware, software, and embedded microcontrollers in noncomputer equipment, such as HVAC security systems, etc.); (b) remediation of the Year 2000 problem (repair, replacement, or retiring of systems); (c) testing of corrected systems (both on a unit level and as a complete enterprise-wide computer system); and, (d) deployment of tested systems into the "live" production environment. I recommend that companies adopt an enterprise-wide *risk management* approach rather than merely a technical remediation approach in attempting to solve the enterprise's Y2K problem.

Dependency Models

Since enterprises face technical risks both from noncompliant internal systems and from noncompliant systems affecting the performance of outside infrastructure (telephone and utility providers, for example) and business partners (central stock brokerage clearinghouses, for example), enterprises often create technical dependency models mapping out both how the enterprise's products and services depend on internal computer systems (internal dependencies) and can be impacted by noncompliancy of third parties (external dependencies). These technical dependency models would be of significantly greater utility to an enterprise if expanded to include business and legal information and factors. Since many enterprises will not have sufficient time prior to January 1, 2000, within which to correct 100 percent of their computer and impacted noncomputer systems, detailed dependency models can assist the enterprise in making more informed triage decisions as to which systems are mission-critical and which are not, both from a technical point of view and from a business/legal point of view. Many enterprises will change over the next few years due to sale and acquisitions of subsidiaries and change in Year 2000 remediation status. Accordingly, it is recommended that the dependency model be contained in a dynamic computer database, rather than in a static paper-based format.

Loss Scenario Analysis

In addition, after the enterprise's technical staff has prepared a list of possible technical loss scenarios, ranked according to magnitude of impact on the enterprise (either on a revenue basis or numerical scale, for example), the above dependency model could be augmented with business and legal risk factors, so as to assist the enterprise in running simulations to determine the likely business and legal impact of each potential technical failure scenario. Top management could then take preventive steps to eliminate or reduce the possible business/legal risk associated with the technical failures most likely to occur and which have the greatest adverse impact on the enterprise.

For example, assume a particular bank uses noncompliant software to issue letters of credit. If the software is unsuccessfully corrected, a letter of credit might be issued with an issuance date of 1999, but an expiration date of 1901, rather than 2001. If the letter of credit is presented in the year 2000 for payment, the bank could be in the catch–22 position of being sued by the customer for honoring an expired letter of credit or being sued by the beneficiary for refusing to honor a letter of credit which obviously was meant to expire in 2001, but was issued mistakenly with a 1901 expiration date due to the Y2K problem. If this potential loss scenario is identified prior to the year 2000, the bank could consider whether it could simply amend its letter of credit application form to require the customer to pre-authorize the bank to reissue letters of credit if mistakenly issued with the wrong expiration date due to the Y2K problem. This would be a "preventive law" approach to the Y2K problem.

Two Key Risks: Third-Party Dependencies and the Y2K "Perception" Problem

Over the past year, I have consulted with numerous large corporations in the financial services industry. For the most part, these corporations are quite confident that they will successfully complete their Year 2000 remediation efforts and make their internal computer systems fully Year 2000 compliant. However, many of these same corporations are less confident about two risks which they face: (a) disruptions to their businesses due to the failure of smaller business partners and other third parties which fail to become compliant in time; and, (b) for public companies, the possibility that their shareholders may "short" their stock due to unfounded fears, fueled by "doomsday" articles in the press, that the companies will not become compliant in time.

Third-Party Dependency Risk

Dealing with the first of the above two issues, enterprises should consider the possibility that they may become involved in litigation due to the failures of business partners to become compliant. For example, a third-party service bureau to a bank may fail to perform processing contracted by the bank due to the service provider's computer systems failing as a result of the Y2K problem. The bank then may be unable to perform its contractual obligations to its customers as a result of the service provider's breach.

An additional risk, however, is that the enterprise may become a defendant in litigation against its business partners where the cause of the business partner's computer system failure is unclear. In some cases, plaintiffs' attorneys may not be able at the outset of litigation to determine why a defendant's computer systems suffered a "hard" crash or "soft" crash and will have to assume that third parties which share data or software with the defendant may have contributed to the computer system failure. Due to applicable statutes of limitation and the desire of the plaintiff to seek joint and several liability from all defendants in case the primary defendant files for bankruptcy, the plaintiff's attorneys are likely to sue not only the primary defendant, but also any business partner which conceivably could have played a part in the system failure due to the sharing of contaminated data or software. The plaintiff's counsel will then seek to sort out the causes of the system failure during the discovery period.

To a third-party defendant enterprise, this may constitute "nuisance" litigation, but it could represent a quite serious risk, nonetheless. Defendants should be mindful that where the outcome of a trial hinges on the functioning of a complex computer system, the trial can become a very expensive exercise in witness testimony, often conflicting, in front of a jury which may be essentially computer-illiterate. If at the time of trial the Year 2000 problem has resulted in serious personal injuries in the society at large due to malfunctioning hospital equipment, air traffic control systems, or has resulted in the delayed mailing of Government benefit checks or to higher unemployment due to increased bankruptcies, some juries may be predisposed to the plaintiff's position. Plaintiff's counsel may also point out that the Y2K problem has been known for decades and yet the defendant did not begin actual corrective work until late in the 1990's, arguing that this is evidence of a reckless disregard for the problem. "After all," plaintiff's counsel may say to the jury, "it's only a matter of going from two digits to four digits. How hard could that be? There must be gross negligence here."

Creation of Due-Diligence Record

In light of the above potential scenario, enterprises should take all necessary steps to create a due-diligence record which could be introduced into evidence in litigation, if necessary, to show that the enterprise acted in good faith, using commercially reasonable efforts to solve its Year 2000 problem. As part of this effort, the enterprise should review its Year 2000 corrective plan against currently available industry metrics as to remediation and testing costs and methods in order to confirm that the plan adopted by the enterprise matches the current industry best practices. As part of this effort, the enterprise could seek to obtain certification of its Year 2000 corrective plan under the ITAA*2000 program, as was recently done by BankBoston. Alternatively, the enterprise could undergo a Year 2000 audit, either in conjunction with applying for Year 2000 insurance or independent of such insurance.

The enterprise could also utilize its Year 2000 remediation plan, if augmented by regular reports generated by project management software showing actual implementation of the remediation plan (together with disclosure of the enterprise's Year 2000 program in the enterprise's annual reports and quarterly reports filed with the U.S. Securities and Exchange Commission, if required), to help establish a "due-diligence" defense under applicable Federal securities laws. In addition, the above documentation could help establish a defense for the enterprise's board of directors under the applicable State Business Judgment Rule, which typically provides that a board of directors is not liable for business judgments made in good faith in the best interests of the enterprise, unless the plaintiff can establish that the board acted with gross negligence. Of course, a board of directors which is uninformed and uninvolved with respect to an enterprise's Year 2000 project, may be barred from relying on the Business Judgment Rule and may be liable in subsequent shareholder suits, in some States, if shown to be guilty of simple negligence.

Crafting an Enterprise Definition of Y2K Compliancy/Termination of Noncompliant Business Partners

An enterprise should not make its Year 2000 situation worse by buying or leasing new computer hardware or licensing new software which is not Y2K compliant. Accordingly, the enterprise should determine what definition of "Year 2000 compliancy" best fits the enterprise and obtain warranties from third-party vendors that new hardware and software being supplied to the enterprise is, in fact, Year 2000 compliant. The enterprise should also be alert to any claims it may have against third-party vendors or consultants under product liability, negligence, fraud, or similar claims, with specific identification of the date by which lawsuits must be filed in order not to be barred under applicable statutes of limitation. Looking forward to the enterprise's Year 2000 "event horizons," when computer systems will begin to fail, which could in some cases be earlier than January 1, 2000, the enterprise should analyze whether it has the contractual right to terminate business contracts with key suppliers and/or distributors or other contract parties which clearly will not become fully compliant in time, based perhaps on the grounds of anticipatory breach, without exposing the enterprise itself to breach of contract liability.

Not Losing the Forest for the Trees

An essential part of implementing a Year 2000 risk management program (as contrasted to a purely technical Year 2000 remediation approach) is to give top management the tools and methodology necessary to systematically identify the key Y2K technical, business, and legal risks facing the enterprise and reduce or eliminate those, rather than spend excessive amounts of time and money chasing illusory or minor problems. One element of this is to adopt a centralized approach to the Year 2000 problem, with informed involvement of top management (the CEO, the CIO, the CFO, the internal auditor, and the risk manager, for example), with a defined hierarchy of responsibility for the Y2K project, with accountability. This type of coordination can help an enterprise avoid simple risk management mistakes, such as the failure to coordinate the enterprise's Year 2000 contingency plans with the enterprise's existing enterprise-wide disaster recovery plan.

Handling the Y2K "Perception Problem"

Centralized direction with the involvement of top management can also help the enterprise devise steps to maintain good shareholder relations so that the shareholders do not "short" the company's stock due to unfounded Y2K worries. These steps might include development of standard enterprise-wide disclosure language for SEC filings, press releases, and shareholder communications, as well as creation of a rapid response team to handle press inquiries if Y2K-based system problems arise. The enterprise could also consider using Y2K audit reports and the securing of Y2K insurance as additional tools for reassuring shareholders that the enterprise is at low risk of a Year 2000 failure.

The above discussion highlights just some of the major elements of what characterizes a strong Year 2000 risk management program. The critical point to be made is that public companies which become the targets of hostile takeovers recognize that they are in a "bet the company" situation which requires full board of directors and top management involvement, extensive business and financial advice and contingency planning. Unfortunately, too few companies currently appear to recognize that the Year 2000 computer problem poses a potentially more significant "bet the company" situation, since in the Y2K environment, there are no extensions of time for additional analysis—the January 1, 2000 deadline is immovable.

How the Federal Government Can Help the Private Sector

Congress can be of considerable assistance to the financial services industry in its efforts to solve its Y2K problem and also promote fuller disclosure of Y2K issues and information. The analysis and the refinement of exactly what form this Governmental help could take would require a considerable effort requiring a joint Governmental/private sector collaboration—one of the reason I have supported Senator Moynihan's S.22 bill to create a National Commission on the Year 2000 Computer Problem to explore this issue, among others. This section of my Prepared Testimony will instead focus on one critical way which the Federal Government could assist the financial services industry: By enacting Year 2000 litigation "safe harbor" for financial services institutions which make a good faith effort to become fully Year 2000 compliant and cooperate in industry-wide Y2K information sharing as requested by appropriate regulatory authorities. Of course, the Y2K litigation "safe harbor" could be expanded for the benefit of companies outside of the financial services sector, in the discretion of Congress.

Y2K Litigation "Safe Harbor"

Dr. Edward Yardeni, Chief Economist with Deutsche Morgan Grenfell, has estimated that a recession may occur by the Year 2000 due, in part, to the Year 2000 computer problem. (*See* Topical Study #37, "New Era Recession? Deflation, Irrational Exuberance & Y2K," at the Internet URL of "http://www.yardeni.com/cyber.html.") In light of the complexity of the Y2K problem and the potentially severe impact it may have on the U.S. economy from a technical and business point of view, it is advisable that financial institutions in the private sector be encouraged to share information as to Year 2000 compliancy status, remediation techniques which they have found helpful, and Y2K risks which they discover.

However, due to fears of providing plaintiffs' attorneys with litigation "ammunition," financial institutions may be reluctant to engage in industry-wide Y2K information sharing or joint remediation efforts. This fear of litigation exposure is heightened due to the potential imposition of punitive damages on defendants. That punitive damages have become a significant factor in jury awards and that the threat of punitive damages may strongly affect a corporation's business decisions is now evident. (*See* Moller, Pace & Carroll, *Punitive Damages in Financial Injury Jury Verdicts* (RAND 1997); see also, Prepared Statement of Theodore Olson before the U.S. Senate Committee on the Judiciary, July 24, 1997.)

In order to encourage financial institutions to become fully compliant and to share necessary information with other institutions, I recommend that this Subcommittee consider introducing legislation to provide a "safe harbor" from punitive damages for financial institutions which establish that they have made a good faith effort to become Year 2000 compliant and which cooperate with industry-wide sharing of Y2K information as may be requested by appropriate regulatory authorities. The demonstration of a good faith effort to become Year 2000 compliant could be made by a national bank, for example, by passing a Year 2000 compliancy audit conducted by the Office of the Comptroller of the Currency. In his testimony before this Subcommittee on July 30, 1997, Eugene A. Ludwig, the Comptroller of the Currency indicated that the OCC, indeed, planned to conduct Y2K examinations of national banks and their service vendors by mid-1998, with follow-up exams where necessary. For financial institutions where no Federal regulatory authority has planned to conduct extensive Y2K audits, a quasi-governmental entity could be established to conduct the audits. This quasi-public entity could be established by Congress, for example, using COMSAT as a model. (*See e.g., Communications Satellite Act,* 76 Stat. 423, 47 U.S.C. Section 731 (1962).)

Why Punitive Damages Are Inappropriate in the Y2K Situation

A strong case can be made that punitive damages are inappropriate in Y2K litigation, in any event. At the time of the writing of the U.S. Constitution, punitive damages were applied in cases of intentional torts, such as assault and battery, libel and slander, and other malicious offenses. Today, punitive damages have been applied to a vastly larger body of offenses. However, even today punitive damages are imposed to punish reprehensible conduct and to deter future others from similar behavior. (*See e.g.,* Schwartz and Behrens, "Punitive Damages Reform," 42 Am. U.L. Rev. 1365 (1993).) This simply does not apply to the Year 2000 computer problem. As Dr. Leon Kappelman has demonstrated, the use by programmers of two digits rather than four digits in year date fields was necessary in past years to save expensive computer memory. Dr. Kappelman calculates that over the past 35 years, companies have saved far more in computer memory costs than they will spend on Y2K remediation and, therefore, the use of two digits rather than four digits for year date fields constituted good business judgment. (*See* Dr. Leon Kappelman, "Accrued Savings of the Year 2000 Problem," in L. Kappelman, *Year 2000 Problem: Strategies and Solutions from the Fortune 100* (Thomson Computer Press 1997) at p. 53.) The Y2K problem, therefore, did not arise from reprehensible conduct. Further, since the Y2K problem is a one-time occurrence, imposing punitive damages on an individual defendant in Y2K litigation will not serve any deterrence function whatsoever, either with respect to the specific defendant or to other potential defendants.

Absent Congressional legislation capping Y2K punitive damages, defendants will be reduced to arguing that Y2K punitive damages awards violate the Due Process Clause of the Fourteenth Amendment to the U.S. Constitution. (*See e.g., Pacific Mutual Life Insurance Co.* v. *Haslip,* 111 S. Ct. 1032 (1991) and *BMW of North America, Inc.* v. *Gore,* 116 S. Ct. 1589 (1996).) Since this relief cannot be assured, companies will likely not share Y2K information fully on an industry-wide basis, due to concerns over Y2K litigation risks. In some States, such as Connecticut and

California, insurance is not permitted to cover extracontractual awards for punitive damages directly assessed against the tortfeasor. (*See e.g.*, Mealey's Litigation Reports, "Insurability of Punitives Issue in Award Challenge," June 25, 1997.) For companies in this uninsured position with respect to punitive damages, it makes it even more unlikely that the companies will participate in industry-wide disclosure or joint remediation programs.

If Congress decides that a complete elimination of punitive damages as a remedy is unwarranted, a lesser solution could be chosen by limiting punitive damage awards to a multiple of compensatory damages awarded. For example, the American College of Trial Lawyers has suggested one possible approach to punitive damage award limitation is to limit punitive damages to two times the amount of compensatory damages awarded, or $250,000, whichever is greater. (*See e.g.*, American College of Trial Lawyers, *Report on Punitive Damages of the Committee on Special Problems in the Administration of Justice*, 13–15 (1989).)

Statutory Precedent for a Y2K "Safe Harbor"

Congress has the authority to enact a "safe harbor" for Y2K litigation eliminating punitive damages since Y2K litigation, even if not as severe as predicted by the Giga Information Group, could constitute a very real burden on interstate commerce. Congress has enacted legislative caps on litigation damages in other similar cases which compare favorably to the Y2K situation, such as in: (a) *The Volunteer Protection Act of 1997* (Pub. L. 105–19); (b) *The Private Securities Litigation Reform Act of 1995* (Pub. L. 104–76); (c) *The Asset Conservation, Lender Liability, and Deposit Insurance Protection Act of 1996* (Pub. L. 104–208); and, (d) *The Price-Anderson Amendments to the Atomic Energy Act of 1954*.

Additional aspects of a Y2K litigation "safe harbor" could be considered, including: (a) the prohibition of liability for noneconomic "pain and suffering" losses; (b) elimination of joint and several liability in favor of a proportionate liability standard; (c) a required determination by the court as to whether the plaintiff's cause of action is frivolous, with the imposition of reasonable attorney's fees and costs if determined to be frivolous; and/or, (d) a requirement that the plaintiff establish proof by "clear and convincing evidence" rather than merely by a "preponderance of the evidence."

Conclusion

The Year 2000 computer problem poses significant litigation risks for many financial services institutions, not necessarily because they themselves will fail to become Year 2000 compliant, but because: (a) they may be affected by the failures of third-party business partners to become fully Year 2000 compliant; or, (b) they may become the object of "strike suits" under Federal securities laws after their stock price drops due to unfounded shareholder concerns about the enterprise's Y2K status, fueled by "doomsday" articles in the press. As a critical part of the U.S. infrastructure, the financial services industry *must* become Year 2000 compliant if severe disruptions to the economy are to be avoided. If financial institutions adopt a comprehensive Y2K risk management approach rather than merely a technical remediation approach, they should be better able to identify and reduce their technical, business, and legal Y2K risks, not only as individual institutions, but also as an industry. In this effort, open disclosure by financial institutions of Y2K compliancy status to their counterpart financial partners, sharing of remediation techniques, and other information sharing would aid in the industry-wide Y2K effort. The financial industry's justifiable concerns over attracting punitive damage awards due to such disclosures makes it imperative that Congress consider enacting legislation creating a Y2K litigation "safe harbor" shielding financial institutions from excessive litigation risks, provided the institutions make a good faith effort to become Year 2000 compliant and participate in industry-wide sharing of Y2K information, as requested by appropriate regulatory authorities.

Mr. Chairman and distinguished Members of the Subcommittee, that concludes my testimony and I would be pleased to address any questions you may have.

EARN MCLE CREDIT: Building an Employment Law Case • Page 39

Los Angeles Lawyer

JUNE 1997, VOL. 20, NO. 4 / $3.00

Litigating
the Year 2000
Computer Problem

Local Rules
for CEQA Cases

The Necessity
Defense

PLUS

**Computer
Counselor:**
Marketing on
the Internet

**Protecting
Your Claim on the
Electronic Frontier**

Former Los Angeles lawyers
David A. Makman and
Joseph F. von Sauers analyze
the emerging intellectual
property law of the Internet

By Jeff Jinnett

The Millennium Strikes Back

*The year **2000** computer problem raises a host of litigation issues for potential plaintiffs and defendants alike*

In recent months, both the legal and general business press have speculated heavily that the so-called Year 2000 computer problem will generate considerable litigation.[1] Capers Jones, chairman of Software Productivity Research, a provider of software measurement, assessment, and estimation products and services, has estimated that for every $1 not spent on repairing the Year 2000 problem, the cost of litigation and potential damages will probably amount to more than $10.[2] Since estimates for correcting the problem range from J.P. Morgan's $200 billion[3] to the Gartner Group estimate of $300 billion to $600 billion,[4] this would result in estimated litigation expenses of several trillion dollars if the necessary corrective work is not done. Thus, the estimate of Giga Information Group, an information technology advisory firm, that Year 2000 litigation costs will be in the $1 trillion range may actually be conservative.[5] The enormity of such costs is underscored by the fact that they would exceed by many times the estimated $300 billion total annual direct and indirect cost of all civil litigation in the United States.[6]

Still, these figures are pure speculation. The actual litigation costs that will result from the Year 2000 computer problem remain unknown because no substantial litigation has yet been reported on the Year 2000 problem and we do not know how much necessary corrective work will ultimately not be completed on time.

The only thing that seems clear is that litigation is inevitable, if only because much of the corrective work simply will not be completed on time. The Gartner Group has estimated that as many as one half of the companies with a Year 2000 problem will not become fully Year 2000 compliant by January 1, 2000.[7] The reasons for this high failure rate are varied: 1) too many companies are starting too late;[8] 2) they are not devoting sufficient personnel and funds to the effort;[9] 3) there are not enough trained programmers available, in any event, to fix all of the software code requiring correction;[10] 4) not enough time and resources will be devoted to the testing phase, which could be the most expensive and time-consuming phase for many companies;[11] 5) even if a particular company becomes fully compliant, its systems may become contaminated by data or software supplied by outside third parties who have not become compliant;[12] and 6) the city or geographic area in which the company has its offices may not have Year 2000 compliant telecommunication and electric utility systems, resulting in infrastructure failures.[13]

The failure of any large percentage of corporate computer systems will have a cascading effect. First will come business dislocations such as breached contracts, delivery of defective products and services, industrial accidents, and business interruptions. These events may, in turn, cause stock prices of affected public companies to fall, which may lead to shareholder derivative suits against the affected companies' boards of directors alleging breach of fiduciary duty and failure to disclose the Year 2000 problem fully in the annual and quarterly reports filed with the U.S. Securities and Exchange Commission.[14]

Affected companies may then sue the computer consultants that had advised them

---

Jeff Jinnett is of counsel to the law firm of LeBoeuf, Lamb, Greene & MacRae, L.L.P., in New York, practicing in the area of computer law. He also serves as president of LeBoeuf Computing Technologies, L.L.C., a business subsidiary of LLG&M engaged in Year 2000 business consulting.

on the design of their computer systems and also sue the vendors that sold, licensed, or maintained the hardware and software in the noncompliant system. Ultimately, many of the entities sued will seek to recover litigation costs from their professional errors and omissions insurance, directors and officers (D&O) liability insurance, and other policies.

These litigation risks are not fanciful, and they are being taken seriously. Several insurance companies are currently undertaking an evaluation of the potential litigation risk that the Year 2000 problem poses to their insurance portfolios. For example, a major insurer recently sent a "Year 2000 Supplemental Questionnaire" to insureds in its D&O liability portfolio, querying whether the insured 1) has inventoried its hardware and software for Year 2000 compliance; 2) has a Year 2000 corrective plan in place; 3) has had its legal counsel review license agreements and long-term maintenance agreements to determine if the vendors of third-party licensed software have an obligation to make their software Year 2000 compliant; 4) has contacted its critical suppliers in order to determine the suppliers' Year 2000 compliance plans; and 5) has a plan to monitor the critical suppliers' progress in becoming Year 2000 compliant.

Insurance companies are likely to send out similar questionnaires under their professional-liability and errors-and-omissions policies in the near future. If an insurance company determines that the risk of the Year 2000 problem to its portfolio is severe, it can consider several corrective steps or combination of steps. It may amend its policies to exclude liabilities arising out of the Year 2000 problem. It could increase premiums to reflect the increased risk. Or, it might refuse to renew coverage for companies that appear not to be serious about becoming Year 2000 compliant on a timely basis.

It is likely that many insurance carriers will take the position that the Year 2000 problem is not a "fortuitous event" covered under business interruption insurance.[15] This gap in business interruption coverage has prompted some insurers to bring new products to the market. For example, Marsh & McLennan, Inc. has announced the creation of a $200 million risk transfer Year 2000 insurance product, and AIG has created a $100 million finite risk Year 2000 insurance product.[16]

There is no lack of potential plaintiffs in Year 2000 litigation. Private sector companies, shareholders of companies, third-party intellectual property owners, customers (individually or as a class[17]), tenants, and governmental entities form only a partial list. Potential defendants include product vendors, consultants, outsourcing vendors, maintenance vendors, contract parties, banks, stock brokerage firms, service providers, boards of directors and top management, building owners of "smart" buildings providing telecommunications service, and governmental entities.

While most litigation is unlikely to commence until after January 1, 2000, since that is the date on which most of the affected systems will begin to fail, some suits may arise earlier. For example, businesses may claim that purchased or licensed software and/or hardware was not Year 2000 compliant as warranted, or that long-term maintenance providers or data-processing outsourcing providers should absorb part or all of the plaintiffs' corrective costs. Other early claims for damages may arise due to the malfunction of noncompliant software applications that conduct forward-looking calculations.[18]

Of course, potential plaintiffs will need to determine if a statute of limitations bars their suits if they wait too long to file.[19] For example, if a plaintiff intends to sue a vendor for selling computer hardware that is not Year 2000 compliant, claiming that the product was defective and breached an implied warranty of merchantability or an express warranty within the sales contract, a four-year contract statute of limitations may apply under Section 2-725(1) of the relevant state's Uniform Commercial Code (UCC). Under Section 2-725(2) of the Uniform Laws Annotated version of the UCC, the cause of action accrues when the breach occurs (i.e., when tender of the goods occurs), regardless of the aggrieved party's lack of knowledge of the breach. However, where a warranty explicitly extends to future performance of the goods and discovery of the breach must await the time of such performance, the cause of action accrues when the breach is or should have been discovered.

A very cautious plaintiff's attorney may decide that the statute began to run when the computer hardware was delivered, rather than when the plaintiff first learned that the hardware was not Year 2000 compliant or at the date of the first failure of the hardware. The plaintiff would then file suit within four years from the date of delivery of the hardware.[20] In some instances, the default statute of limitations may have been shortened by contractual agreement of the parties.[21]

Among potential defendants,

hardware and software vendors and service providers face perhaps the greatest exposure. Among the causes of action that plaintiffs may bring against them are:

Breach of an express warranty that a product is Year 2000 compliant. Since there is no single, uniformly accepted legal definition of what it means for a product to be Year 2000 compliant, these suits may require the court to choose between competing definitions of compliancy put forth by the plaintiff and the defendant.[22]

Breach of an express warranty by the vendor that the software contained no viruses. Plaintiffs may argue that the Year 2000 "millennium bug" constitutes a "logic bomb"—a debilitating software code akin to a virus that activates itself at a specified date or time—in breach of an express warranty that the software was virus free.[23] Plaintiffs could, alternatively, argue that the vendor's disclaimer of implied warranty or merchantability was ineffective to exclude liability for latent defects such as a logic bomb, since to permit such a disclaimer would be unconscionable.[24]

Negligent misrepresentation or fraud. Plaintiffs may offer the theory that the vendor knew that the plaintiff intended to utilize the product into the next century and fraudulently failed to alert the plaintiff to the fact that the product would not operate properly past its first "event horizon," which might even precede January 1, 2000.[25]

"Failure of essential remedy" under the license agreement. Where the computer products are considered "goods" within that state's UCC,[26] a vendor's disclaimer of other remedies (implied warranties and consequential damages, for example) should be deemed ineffective, if the vendor's only offered remedy is to repair the defects, and the vendor fails to do so successfully.[27]

Violation of a state deceptive trade practices law.[28]

Fraudulent misrepresentation. Plaintiffs may offer the theory that the vendor's advertising implied that all of its products would be made Year 2000 compliant, when in fact the vendor had decided secretly not to provide Year 2000 compliant upgrades for older versions of its hardware and/or software. Instead, the vendor made only its most recent versions compliant in order to force its customers to upgrade.[29]

Tort claims for personal injury or property damages based on negligent misrepresentation, fraud, or strict product liability.[30] Note that some courts are reluctant to allow claims for pure economic loss under a tort theory, preferring to restrict the theory to cases involving personal injury and/or property damage.[31]

Claims for injunctive relief. Plaintiffs may seek injunctions against vendors that refuse to grant access to the source code of a licensed program so that the licensee may modify the software to make it Year 2000 compliant.

Violation of criminal laws. Plaintiffs

may allege that laws prohibiting the marketing of a "destructive computer program" have been violated.[32]

Failure to comply with an agreement. A vendor's refusal to correct the Year 2000 defect as part of an existing long-term maintenance or outsourcing agreement may be actionable.[33]

Consultants who advised businesses in the installation of hardware and/or software may also find themselves defendants in litigation. Plaintiffs may bring suit against consultants under any of the following causes of action:

Negligence. The failure to design Year 2000 compliant computer systems may constitute actionable negligence, and the failure to warn the plaintiff of a Year 2000 problem may be deemed negligent misrepresentation.[34]

Failure to exercise "good faith and fair dealing." Plaintiffs may charge that consultants wrongfully failed to disclose the Year 2000 compliancy problem as part of consultation in the purchase of a computer product.[35]

Malpractice. The design of a computer system that became obsolete due to the Year 2000 problem may constitute professional malpractice in some cases.[36]

The Year 2000 problem may eventually reach corporate boardrooms as shareholders bring suits against boards of directors and top management. These suits might include charges of 1) waste of corporate assets;[37] 2) breach of fiduciary duty, duty of due care, and/or duty of loyalty;[38] 3) securities law violations;[39] and 4) breach of duties under federal and state banking laws, pension laws (e.g., ERISA), and similar laws.[40]

The actual behavior of many companies in addressing the problem will allow some plaintiffs to accuse a defendant company's directors and top management of gross negligence and reckless disregard of their duty of due care. Consider the situation in which a company's directors and management may have been aware of the Year 2000 problem for decades, but waited far too long to begin actual corrective work, did not hold a single board of directors meeting on the Year 2000 problem, and did not even approve a budget for the corrective work, expecting that the company's information systems staff would be able to resolve the problems within its existing maintenance budget. This, plaintiffs may

The Year 2000 problem may eventually reach boardrooms as shareholders bring suits against top management.

charge, inevitably led to a failure of the company's Year 2000 corrective plan.

While vendors, consultants, and top company directors and management may face the greatest exposure to Year 2000 lawsuits, the fallout may eventually reach a large number of other potential defendants. For example, software licensees may be sued for infringement of the intellectual property rights of a licensor if their corrective action includes the reverse engineering of software, in breach of their license agreements, in order to modify the source code to make it Year 2000 compliant.[41] Manufacturers of noncomputer equipment (such as HVAC systems, elevators, security systems, and consumer products) may face product liability claims, including personal injury and property damage claims, if the equipment was manufactured with noncompliant embedded microchips.[42]

The effort to find solutions to the Year 2000 problem may lead employers of software programmers to "raid" their competitors

in order to obtain sufficient human resources. This may result in allegations of misappropriation of trade secrets and tortious interference with a competitor's business.[43]

Others that may face suits include banks, stock brokerage firms, and similar entities for monies lost due to improper or failed financial transactions, stock trades, settlements, etc.[44] Landlords of "smart" buildings may be sued for breach of the lease covenant of quiet enjoyment, based on the failure of the landlord to provide telecommunications service for the tenant's computer systems due to the malfunction of the building telephone PBX caused by the Year 2000 problem.[45]

And, of course, insurers will almost certainly face coverage actions. Some insureds will argue that the business interruption damages suffered due to the Year 2000 problem should be covered under the insured's business interruption insurance despite the insurer's position that the Year 2000 problem does not constitute an insurable "fortuitous event."[46] Directors and officers will argue that the D&O liability policy should cover suits arising out of a Year 2000 problem, despite the insureds' failure to disclose the Year 2000 problem in insurance applications or renewal applications, or the insurer's position that no "claims" had been made during the policy period.[47]

Defendants in professional malpractice or negligence actions may claim that an insurer wrongfully failed to honor claims against a professional errors and omissions policy.[48] And there will also likely be claims that the insurer wrongfully terminated or failed to renew the insured's professional errors and omissions insurance, D & O insurance, or business interruption insurance.[49]

Damages sought by plaintiffs in litigation could include direct, indirect, incidental, special, consequential, and punitive damages, as well as recovery of fines and penalties assessed by governmental agencies. It should be recognized, however, that some types of damages may be unavailable due to 1) the parties to a transaction having agreed to exclude them;[50] 2) exclusion by operation of statute;[51] 3) exclusion by operation of a tariff, for example, in the case of a telephone company;[52] or 4) the reluctance of a court to award punitive damages in a contract dispute.[53]

Against this multipronged

offensive by plaintiffs, defendants will have a variety of defenses available. Some potential defenses may have very broad application and be available to several types of defendants. For example a statute of limitations may bar many plaintiff claims.[54] Other plaintiff claims may be barred by the disclaimer-of-warranties and limitation-of-remedies language in the contract.[55] In many cases a defendant may be able to argue that it was following industry standard practice in designing computer systems, writing software, and/or manufacturing microchips using two-digit year-date fields, and that this practice has been shown to be reasonable on a cost-benefit, historical analysis.[56]

Other defenses will depend more narrowly on the relationship of plaintiff and defendant. For example, vendor defendants will be able to argue that the plaintiff assumed the risk of a Year 2000 problem and is estopped from raising its claim. In other words, the defendant may argue that the plaintiff customer must have known about the Year 2000 problem when it purchased the hardware or software, since this problem has been common knowledge in the technology community for decades.[57]

A defendant supplier may argue that it is not liable under the theory of "force majeure" for the breach of its contract with plaintiff. The defendant may claim that it was unable to perform because one of its own suppliers caused a Year 2000 problem, and this failure was not anticipated by the defendant and was beyond the defendant's reasonable control.[58]

Company boards of directors and/or officers who find themselves defendants may have a "due diligence" defense to the plaintiffs' securities law violation claim.[59] Defendant's directors and/or officers may also argue that they are not liable under the applicable state's "business judgment rule," unless plaintiffs can prove that the defendants are guilty of fraud, bad faith, abuse of discretion, of being uninformed, or guilty of gross negligence.[60]

Governmental entities may rely on the defense of sovereign immunity, subject to applicable tort claims acts.[61]

In many areas of the law,

default rules have been developed through case law decisions, statutory provisions, and industry custom. These default rules may yield unintended results when applied to Year 2000 noncompliancy situations. In those cases, it would be best to determine whether preventive measures can be taken to minimize potential damages if litigation occurs.

For example, if a bank uses software to generate letters of credit, and the software is not made Year 2000 compliant, letters of credit intended to expire in the year 2001 may indicate an expiration date of 1901. If the recipient of the letter of credit has agreed to accept letters of credit in electronic form, the discrepancy may not be immediately noticed. At a subsequent date, when the letter of credit is presented for payment, the customer (that is, the party that purchased the letter of credit) may demand that the letter not be honored, since the letter of credit has already technically expired. Under UCC Section 5-106,[62] if there is no stated expiration date or other provision that determines its duration, a letter of credit expires one year after its stated date of issuance, or if none is stated, after the date on which it is issued. The bank may decide 1) that the customer actually intended the letter of credit to have an expiration date of 2001 and honor the letter of credit on that basis; 2) that the letter of credit should be considered under UCC Section 5-106 as having no expiration date and treat it as a one-year letter of credit; or 3) to refuse to honor the letter of credit, since it was defectively issued, and the customer had refused to authorize a revision to the document.

Whatever course of action the bank takes, it risks being sued for wrongful honor or wrongful dishonor of the letter of credit. Rather than face this situation, the issuing bank could examine the possibility of amending its standard letter of credit application to provide that the customer agrees that any letter of credit issued with an incorrect expiration date due to a Year 2000 computer problem may be reissued with the accurate date by the issuing bank based on the initial customer application.

Another example of a preventive law measure would apply to electronic data interchange (EDI) transactions. The default rule in EDI transactions, unless the parties have agreed otherwise, is that the sender of an EDI message is responsible for the loss incurred if the value-added network (VAN) does not accurately transmit a message to the intended EDI recipient.[63] This default rule may be reasonable when the occurrence of a VAN mistake is rare, but if a VAN fails to become Year 2000 compliant and incorrectly transmits thousands of EDI messages, the VAN may file for bankruptcy and fail to indemnify all of the various senders for the damages.

Rather than face this problem, EDI senders could amend their trading partner agreements to provide that the sender and recipient share equally in any loss caused by the noncompliance of a VAN, whether chosen by the sender or the recipient. The sender and recipient could also require the VAN to secure Year 2000 insurance, which would not be issued unless the VAN had a satisfactory Year 2000 corrective plan in place and continued to implement its plan through the year 2000.

The Year 2000 litigation issue is complex and difficult. Any list of potential plaintiffs and defendants, causes of action, and defenses is necessarily speculative and not exhaustive. However, it is clearly evident that the potential for Year 2000 litigation is vast.

If the Gartner Group prediction that one half of companies with a Year 2000 problem will fail to become fully compliant is correct, significant litigation is sure to result. In this light, attorneys should advise clients about preventive law steps that could reduce the impact of any Year 2000 litigation. ■

[1] *Responsible?: Who May Be Held Legally Liable for This Problem?* (http://www.y2k.com/whosresp.htm); Wendy Leibowitz, *Lawyers Brace for Countdown and Out to 2000*, THE NATIONAL L.J., Oct. 28, 1996; Sue Mellen, *Protecting Your Company Against Year 2000 Liability* (http:www.dciexpo.com/news/9702/2000legl.htm); Clyde Mitchell, *Implications of the Year 2000 Problem*, NEW YORK L.J., Apr. 16, 1997, at 3; Vito Peraino, *Year 2000 Crisis Poses New Liability Exposures*, NATIONAL UNDERWRITER, Feb. 17, 1997, at 36; Richard Raysman & Peter Brown, *Back to the Future: De-Bugging the "Millennium Bug,"* NEW YORK L.J., Feb. 11, 1997, at 3; Warren Reid, *2001: A Legal Odyssey (The Millennium Bug)*, THE COMPUTER LAWYER, June 1996, at 15; *Lawyers Ponder Y2k Liability Concerns* (ITAA Year 2000 Outlook) Oct. 11, 1996 (http://www.itaa.org/year2000.htm); Adam Taylor, *Millennium Meltdown-The Legal Labyrinth*, INSURANCE SPECIALIST, Jan. 1997, at 48; Saundra Torry, *Marking the Calendar for a Potential Windfall of Zeros*, WASHINGTON POST, Dec. 30, 1996, at F07; Thelen, Marrin, Johnson & Bridges, L.L.P., *The Need for Immediate Action at the Highest Corporate Levels to Solve the Year 2000 Software Crisis* (http://www.comlinks.com/legal/tmjb2.htm); Precana Thompson et al., *Solve Your Year 2000 Problem Now or Risk Being Sued* (http://web.idirect.com/~mbsprog/y2ksue.html).

[2] Capers Jones, *The Global Economic Impact of the Year 2000 Software Problem* (http://www.spr.com/library/y2k00.htm).

[3] William Rabin, *Industry Analysis: The Year 2000 Problem* (http://www.jpmorgan.com/MarketDataInd/Research/Year2000/index .html).

[4] Gartner Group, *"Year 2000 Problem" Gains National Attention* (http://www.gartner.com/aboutgg/pressrel

(Continued on page 58)

The Millennium Strikes Back

(Continued from page 38)

/pry2000.html).

[5] *Hearings before the U.S. House of Representatives Science Committee et al.* (Mar. 20, 1997) (testimony of Ann Coffou, managing director of Giga Information Group) (http://www.itpolicy.gsa.gov/mks/yr2000 /hearing.html); Rex Nutting, *Y2K Could Cost $1 Trillion in Legal Costs*, TechWire, Mar. 20, 1997 (http://www .techweb.com/se/directlink.cgi?WIR1997032014).

[6] Jack Kemp, *Common Good Above Profits*, The National L.J., Nov. 4, 1996, at A20; H. Moskowitz & R. Wallace, *Loser Pays: A Deterrent to Frivolous Claims*, New York L.J., Mar. 7, 1996, at 2; Robert Smith, *Saving Ourselves from Being Lawyered to Death*, Washington Post, Dec. 23, 1996, at C04.

[7] Mark Evans, *The Profit Clock is Ticking on Year 2000 Countdown*, Financial Post, May 8, 1996, at 22; APT Data Services, *Counting the Cost of Year 2000*, Computer Finance, Mar. 1, 1996.

[8] *See* Leon Kappelman, *Mitigating Year 2000 Project Risks* (http://www.year2000.com/archive/mitigating .html).

[9] *Id.*

[10] *See* Capers Jones, *supra* note 2.

[11] *See* Leon Kappelman & James Cappel, *Critical Issue Report: Facing the Year 2000 Problems* (http://www .comlinks.com/mag/cirep.htm).

[12] *See* Leland Freeman & Larry Meador, *Year 2000: The Domino Effect*, Datamation, Jan. 1997, at 40 (http//www.datamation.com/PlugIn/workbench /yr2000/year.htm).

[13] *See* Corporation 2000, *Year 2000 Preparation*, Survive! The Business Continuity Magazine, Nov. 1996, at 10; David Bicknell, *New York City to Raise $4M for Millennium Research*, Computer Weekly, Feb. 20, 1997, at 14; David Bicknell, *Millennium Infrastructure: Urban Worriers*, Computer Weekly (UK), Mar. 20, 1997, at 50-52 (http://www.compinfo.co.uk/y2k /compwk01.htm).

[14] *See* Jeff Jinnett, *Legal Issues Concerning the Year 2000 "Millennium Bug,"* The Computer Lawyer, Dec. 1996, at 16, 20-22 (http://www.year2000.com/archive /NFlegalissues.html); Jeff Jinnett, *Year 2000 Problem: Disclosure Obligations and Impact*, Journal of Lending & Credit Risk Management, Feb. 1997, at 79.

[15] *See* Jeff Jinnett, *Legal Issues Concerning the Year 2000 "Millennium Bug,"* supra note 14, at 24; David Schaefer, *Insurance and Y2K* (http://www.y2k .com/insurqa .htm).

[16] *See Insurers to Offer Policies for Y2K Exposure* (ITAA Year 2000 Outlook), Jan. 31, 1997 (http://www.itaa.org /year2000.htm).

[17] *See, e.g.*, Microsoft Corp. v. Manning, 914 S.W. 2d 602 (Tex. Ct. App. 1995) (affirming certification of a class action based on alleged breach of an express warranty in a mass-market product, Microsoft's MS-DOS 6.0).

[18] *See* Jeff Jinnett, *Legal Issues Concerning the Year 2000 "Millennium Bug,"* supra note 14.

[19] *See* Susan Thomas, Annotation, *Computer Sales and Leases: Time When Cause of Action for Failure of Performance Accrues*, 90 A.L.R. 4th 298 (1996).

[20] *See, e.g.*, Liecar Liquors, Ltd. v. CRS Business Computers Inc., 613 N.Y.S 2d 298 (3d Dept. 1994) (holding that statute of limitations ran from tender of delivery of pen scanner).

[21] *See, e.g.*, Ram Systems of La Crosse, Wisconsin, Inc. v. Wichita Coca-Cola Bottling Co., 1994 U.S. Dist. LEXIS 12566 (D. Kan. 1994) (acknowledging the parties' rights to contractually shorten the applicable statutory period).

[22] *See* Jeff Jinnett, *Legal Issues Confronting the Federal Government and the State Governments Due to the Year 2000 "Millennium Bug"* (http://www.llgm .com/FIRM/article4.htm), under the heading "Year 2000 Compliance Warranties"; *see also* Alois Gross, Annotation, *Computer Sales and Leases: Breach of Warranty, Misrepresentation, or Failure of Consideration as Defense or Ground for Affirmative Relief*, 37 A.L.R. 4th 110 (1996).

[23] Standard definitions of a computer "virus" include the concept that the virus uses the resources of the host computer to replicate itself, possibly in an evolved form, which the Y2K Millennium Bug does not do; *see* F. Cohen, A Short Course on Computer Viruses 2 (2d ed. 1994); the Millenium Bug does resemble a "logic bomb," however, which is often classed with viruses but is not technically a virus since it does not replicate itself. *See* Robert Slade's Guide to Computer Viruses 450 (1994); *but see*, Peter Sakkas, *Espionage and Sabotage in the Computer World*, 5 Int'l J. Intelligence & Counterintelligence 155, 158 (1992) (classifying the logic bomb as a type of virus).

[24] *See, e.g.*, Sierra Diesel Injection Serv., Inc. v. Burroughs Corp., 874 F. 2d 653 (9th Cir. 1989) (finding that warranty disclaimer in computer sales contract was ineffective and holding computer vendor liable for breach of warranty); Restatement (Second) of Contracts §208 (1981) (court may refuse to enforce unconscionable term of contract).

[25] *See* Raymond Nimmer, The Law of Computer Technology §6.07[3] n.98 and n.10.03 (2d ed. 1997); Restatement (Second) of Torts §552(1) (1977); Clements Auto Co. v. Service Bureau Corp., 444 F. 2d 169 (8th Cir. 1971) (holding defendant liable for misrepresentations made in connection with the sale of data processing services.); *see also* Walker, *Computer Litigation and the Manufacturer's Defenses Against*

Fraud, 2 COMPUTER L. REP. 199 (1983).

26 See, e.g., The Colonial Life Ins. Co. v. EDS, 817 F. Supp. 235 (D. N.H. 1993) (applying the UCC to a license agreement for computer software).

27 See, e.g., UCC §2-719(2); Chatlos Sys. v. National Cash Register Corp., 635 F. 2d 1081 (3d Cir. 1980) (holding vendor liable under UCC for sale of faulty computer system but upholding contractual limitation of remedies).

28 See, e.g., Sun Power, Inc. v. Adams, 751 S.W. 2d 689 (Tex. Ct. App. 1988) (finding a "gross disparity [between] the value received and the consideration paid" in the sale of a cash register and finding vendor liable under the deceptive trade practices act); see also VMark Software, Inc. v. EMC Corp., 642 N.E. 2d 587 (Mass. App. 1994) (finding licensor of software liable for misrepresentation and deceptive trade practices); see also UNIFORM DECEPTIVE TRADE PRACTICES ACT, 7A U.L.A. 265 (1966).

29 See, e.g., Advanced Business Sys., Inc. v. Phillips Information Sys. Co., 750 F. Supp. 774 (E.D. La. 1990) (charging vendor with fraud and misrepresentation for promising continued support of U.S. market, but later abandoning market).

30 See, e.g., Lewis v. Timko, Inc., 697 F. 2d 1252 (5th Cir. 1983), modified on reh'g, 746 F. 2d 1425 (applying strict product liability for personal injury caused by defective and unreasonably dangerous computer-controlled hydraulic tongs); Winter v. G.P. Putnam's Sons, 938 F. 2d 1033 (9th Cir. 1991) (noting in dictum that defective software may be a "product" for product liability law purposes).

31 See, e.g., Apollo Group, Inc. v. Avnet, Inc., 58 F. 3d 477 (9th Cir. 1995) (claim for economic losses by computer buyer on negligent misrepresentation cause of action barred); Transport Corp. of Am. Inc. v. IBM, 30 F. 3d 953 (8th Cir. 1994) (economic loss doctrine bars tort claim for loss of data on disk drive). See also Special Committee on Computers and Law, Tort Theories in Computer Litigation, 38 RECORD OF ASS'N OF BAR OF CITY OF N.Y. 426, 427 (1983).

32 See, e.g., Computer Crimes Act, NEB. REV. STAT. §28-1343 (9), (10) (1996) (prohibiting the marketing of a computer program with a "destructive function," which means that it degrades, disables or alters the performance of a computer, its associated peripheral equipment, or a computer program). This type of complaint may be unlikely to be raised with respect to programs marketed in the past, but may be raised against vendors who persist in marketing Year 2000 noncompliant programs to unsuspecting consumers in the future, especially in 1998 and 1999; see also note 23 supra, discussing "logic bombs."

33 See Jeff Jinnett, Legal Issues Concerning the Year 2000 "Millennium Bug," supra note 14.

34 See, e.g., Shell Pipeline Corp. v. Coastal States Trading, Inc., 788 S.W. 2d 837 (Tex. Ct. App. 1990) (claiming negligence in the design of a system for processing of gas orders in connection with a pipeline); see also Invacare Corp. v. Sperry Corp., 612 F. Supp. 448 (N.D. Ohio 1984) (claiming vendor had negligently recommended a particular computer system and inappropriate programs); David Gutter Furs v. Jewelers Protection Servs, Ltd., 79 N.Y. 2d 1027 (1992) (claiming negligent design and configuration of a computerized alarm system).

35 See RESTATEMENT (SECOND) OF CONTRACTS §205 (1981).

36 See, e.g., Diversified Graphics, Ltd. v. Groves, 868 F. 2d 293 (8th Cir. 1989) (finding that computer consultant Ernst & Whinney should be held to a professional standard of care with respect to the selection of a turnkey computer system) (this appears to be a minority view among state courts); but see Hospital Computer Systems, Inc. v. The Staten Island Hospital, 788 F. Supp. 1351, 1361 (D. N.J. 1992) (finding that computer consultants are not "professionals" under New York law so as to support a claim of professional malpractice); see also Data Processing Serv. v. L.H. Smith Oil Corp., 492 N.E. 2d 314 (Ind. App. 1986) (expecting programmer to have reasonable skill and exercise diligence ordinarily possessed by well-informed members of the trade or profession). See also John Fossett, The Development of Negligence in Computer Law, 14 N. KY. L. REV. 289 (1987); Kevin McKinnon, Note, Computer Malpractice, 23 SANTA CLARA L. REV. 1065 (1983); Joseph Tiano, Jr., Comment, The Liability of Computerized Information Providers, 56 U. PITT. L. REV. 655 (1995).

37 See, e.g., Schuylkill Skyport Inn, Inc. v. Rich, 1996 U.S. Dist. LEXIS 12655 (E.D. Pa. 1996); FLETCHER, CYCLOPEDIA OF THE LAW OF PRIVATE CORPORATIONS, §5911.

38 See Model Business Corporation Act, §8.30(a); E. BRODSKY & M. ADAMSKI, LAW OF CORPORATE OFFICERS AND DIRECTORS §2:04 at 2-11, 2-12 (1995).

39 See, e.g., In re Storage Technology Corp. Sec. Litig., 630 F. Supp. 1072 (D. Colo. 1986) (claiming violations of federal securities laws based on allegations that the directors and officers of the company recklessly concealed and misrepresented information about the company's financial status and product developments). For an example of a Year 2000 disclosure in an annual report, see the Form 10-K of Morgan Stanley Group Inc., for the fiscal year ended Nov. 30, 1996 ("Competition Regulation and Certain Risk Factors").

40 See Vito Peraino, Corporate Directors' Liability and the Year 2000 Problem, DELAWARE CORPORATE LITIGATION REPORTER, Feb. 17, 1997, at 19874.

41 See NIMMER, supra note 25, §1.18[3].

42 See, generally, Hearings, supra note 5; National Controls Corporation v. National Semiconductor Corp., 833 F. 2d 491 (3d Cir. 1987) (finding manufacturer liable for breach of contract and warranties after delivering defective microprocessor chips).

43 See, e.g., Telex Corp. v. IBM, 367 F. Supp. 258 (N.D. Okla. 1973), aff'd in part and rev'd in part, 510 F. 2d 894 (10th Cir. 1975), cert. dismissed, 423 U.S. 802 (1975) (finding that Telex misappropriated IBM confidential information and trade secrets by hiring former IBM employees).

44 See, e.g., Banque Worms v. BankAmerica Int'l, 77 N.Y. 2d 362 (1991) (litigating issues arising from an improper wire transfer); Davis v. Merrill Lynch, Pierce, Fenner & Smith, 906 F. 2d 1206 (8th Cir. 1990) (awarding compensatory and punitive damages for unauthorized trading in customer's account; rejecting defendant's argument that plaintiff should have alerted defendant to unauthorized trading after receiving computer-generated account statements).

45 See, e.g., Sugarman et al., Legal Issues Involved in Tenant Telecommunications Services, in SUGARMAN ET AL., THE COMMERCIAL REAL ESTATE TENANT'S HANDBOOK 379 (1987); see, e.g., Blue Cross Ass'n v. 666 North Lake Shore Drive Associates, 427 N.E. 2d 270 (Ill. App. Ct. 1981) (enjoining lessor from making renovations to leased property that disturbed tenant's computer operations).

46 See, e.g., Compagnie Des Bauxites de Guinee v. Insurance Co. of North Am., 554 F. Supp. 1080 (W.D. Pa. 1983) (denying business interruption coverage because an insurer is not liable for losses resultant from inherent defect or infirmity in the subject matter insured).

47 See, e.g., FDIC v. Mijalis, 15 F. 3d 1314 (5th Cir. 1994) (litigating coverage under a D&O insurance policy); COUCH ON INSURANCE §S38:6.

48 See, e.g., USM Corp. v. First State Ins. Co., 641 N.E. 2d 115 (Mass. App. Ct. 1994) (holding consultant's errors and omissions insurance policy covered breach of express warranty to design turnkey computer system).

49 See, e.g., Rozenfeld v. Medical Protective Co., 73 F. 3d

154 (7th Cir. 1986) (discussing duty to disclose potential liability when renewing insurance policy).

See UCC §2-719, which permits the parties to a contract for the sale of "goods" under the UCC to exclude liability for consequential damages; see, e.g., D.S. Am. Inc. v. Chromagratx Imaging Svs., Inc., 873 F. Supp. 786 (E.D. N.Y. 1995) (discussing contractual limitation on consequential damages); Liberty Fin. Mgmt. Corp. v. Beneficial Data Processing Corp., 670 S.W. 2d 40 (Mo. Ct. App. 1984) (upholding contract disclaimer of all but direct damages).

See, e.g., UCC §4A-305, which bars the recovery of "consequential" damages from a receiving bank for its failure to execute a payment order properly.

See, e.g., Lebowitz Jewelers, Ltd. v. New England Tel. and Tel. Co., 508 N.E. 2d 125 (Mass. App. Ct. 1987) (limiting liability of defendant based on regulations governing its public utility tariff).

But see The Glovatorium, Inc. v. NCR Corp., 684 F. 2d 658 (9th Cir. 1982) (affirming an award of punitive damages against computer vendor for intentional misrepresentation of computer system's performance).

See Nelson, *The 1990 Federal "Fallback" Statute of Limitations: Limitations by Default*, 72 NEB. L. REV. 454 (1983); Comment, *Developments in the Law-Statutes of Limitations*, 63 HARV. L. REV. 1178 (1950); Comment, *A Comprehensive Statute of Limitations for Litigation Arising from Defective Computer Systems*, 37 STAN. L. REV. 1539 (1985).

See, e.g., ADP Credit Corp. v. H.M. Coby Associates, 1990 U.S. Dist. LEXIS 16575 (E.D. N.Y. 1990) (recognizing a UCC disclaimer of warranties as a bar to lawsuit).

See, e.g., Leon Kappelman, *Accrued Savings of the Year 2000 Computer Date Problem* (http://www.comlinks.com/mag/acer.html).

See, e.g., IVARS PETERSON, FATAL DEFECT: CHASING KILLER COMPUTER BUGS 113-141 (1995); see, e.g., Florida Power & Light Co. v. Westinghouse Electric Co., 826 F. 2d 239, 256 (4th Cir. 1987), cert. denied, 485 U.S. 1021 (1988) (finding that Westinghouse implicitly assumed the risk that technical reprocessing solution with respect to spent uranium fuel would not be available).

See, e.g., Advanced Graphic Applications, Inc. v. R. R. Donnelley & Sons Co., 746 F. Supp. 370 (S.D. N.Y. 1990) (litigating whether an employee strike is a "force majeure" excuse for nonperformance); Port City State Bank v. American National Bank, Lawton, Oklahoma, 486 F. 2d 196 (10th Cir. 1973) (excusing bank from damages due to computer failure because of existence of good-faith disaster recovery plan); *see generally* Burk & Wilner, *Failure to Prepare: Who's Liable in a Data Processing Disaster?*, 5 S.C. COMPUTER & HIGH TECH L.J. 19 (1989).

See, e.g., Securities Act Release No. 6335 (SEC Rule 176; Reasonable Investigation and Reasonable Grounds for Belief under Section 11).

See, e.g., Bane v. Ferguson, 890 F. 2d 11, 11 (7th Cir. 1989) (holding that a partner could not be held liable for dissolution of partnership if action was motivated by good-faith judgment); Unocal Corp. v. Mesa Petroleum Co., 493 A. 2d 946 (Del. 1985) (discussing and applying the business judgment rule); E. BRODSKY & M. ADAMSKI, LAW OF CORPORATE OFFICERS §2:07 (1995).

See, e.g., In re Jove Eng'g, Inc., 92 F. 3d 1539, 1549 (11th Cir. 1996) (discussing and applying the doctrine of sovereign immunity); Peterson & Van Der Weide, *Susceptible Faulty Analysis: United States v. Gaubert and the Resurrection of Federal Sovereign Immunity*, 72 NOTRE DAME L. REV. 447 (1997).

UCC §5-106 (Issuance, Amendment, Cancellation and Duration).

See, e.g., ABA MODEL AGREEMENT, §1.23 in AMERICAN BAR ASSOCIATION, *The Commercial Use of Electronic Data Interchange: A Report and Model Trading Partner Agreement*, 45 BUS. LAW. 1645 (1990); CALAMARI & PERILLO, THE LAW OF CONTRACTS §2-24.

PREPARED STATEMENT OF
DANA D. McDANIEL & GREGORY P. CIRILLO
WILLIAMS, MULLEN, CHRISTIAN & DOBBINS

OCTOBER 22, 1997

Introduction

This summary, and my comments to the Subcommittee, will briefly discuss three aspects of legal liability that businesses face as a result of the Year 2000 or Y2K computer problem. I will discuss business, customer, and shareholder liability issues,[1] and conclude by proposing: (i) Consideration of modest statutory clarifications intended to restore the balance established in the Copyright Act between the rights of copyright owners and their licensees; and, (ii) further study of Federal consumer protection laws to determine whether safe harbor legislation would be appropriate to immunize financial institutions and businesses from liability for procedural violations caused by Year 2000 computer problems—in the absence of actual harm to the consumer.

Liability Assessment

Assessment of Business Liability

The potential for business liability resulting from Year 2000 computer problems is real and significant. Businesses have become extremely interdependent as a result of the trend toward outsourcing, teaming, and just-in-time delivery systems. As a result, the failure or slowdown of a single link in a production and distribution chain can generate multiple levels of harm and liability. Possible scenarios are easy to imagine. For example, the failure or the malfunction of an automated inventory system operated by a food product wholesaler could cause that wholesaler to under-supply its distributors, and cause those distributors to under-supply food product retailers. The retailer, in turn, may be left unable to meet its prior supply obligations. Each party in this chain of events may have a legal claim against its predecessor in the chain.

With a few exceptions, however, all of the liabilities arising as a result of these examples are—from a legal standpoint—conventional causes of action; and existing law is well equipped to deal with these claims. There is also no compelling reason to alter existing law to deny any of these parties' compensation for the harm they suffer. In almost all cases, the party who fails to perform without excuse would and should be liable for that breach.

Assessment of Consumer Liability

Retail businesses, including the financial services industry, risk the greatest disruption from Year 2000 computer problems due to the number of potential individuals who would be affected.[2] Lost or inaccurate account balances, incorrect interest charges, and errant notices of default all could result from Year 2000 computer problems. Similarly, providers of consumer services, including utilities, telephone service, and cable television, could face a multitude of small claims resulting from Year 2000 related failures. The good news is that this type of disruption is likely to be temporary and, while frustrating, not likely to cause individual consumers substantial direct damages.[3] Even if damages are incurred, the nature of the claims (high in number and similar in nature, but small in individual dollar amount) suggest that State attorney general actions and private class actions would be effective remedies.

Assessment of Shareholder Liability

It is not unreasonable to expect that Year 2000 computer problems will adversely affect the share price, value, or viability of some publicly traded and closely held corporations.[4] As a result, shareholders may have claims under statutory and/or common law against the corporate directors and officers if the adverse affects were

---

[1] These comments will not discuss the legal claims software users may have against systems vendors for providing a defective or nonconforming product.

[2] Thanks in part to effective Federal regulatory action, the banking and financial industry is well ahead of other industry groups in its Year 2000 remediation efforts. One can only hope that other consumer financial service industries, like credit card providers and investment brokerage services, will follow suit.

[3] Of course, there can be exceptional cases. For example, a multitude of missed or erroneous trades on an institutional level could generate much larger liability.

[4] Inadequate disclosure of the financial impact of the Year 2000 computer problem could also trigger liability under Federal and State securities laws, and the governing rules of securities exchanges.

the result of the failure of those directors and officers to exercise due care in addressing this issue. From the business standpoint, disclosure and prudent management remain the best deterrents to shareholder derivative and similar suits, and the best defense to liability in such suits. These hearings, together with the publicity the Year 2000 computer problem is receiving, will help to ensure that management will be made aware of the problem, and *competent* management teams will have implemented an appropriate Year 2000 Plan.

Recommendations

It is said that bad facts make bad law. The Year 2000 problem raises issues that have never been seen before, and may never be seen again, and legislative efforts to address these issues could yield awkward results and disruptive legal precedent. In addition, while there may be imperfections in our legal systems as they relate to class actions, shareholder derivative actions, and litigation in general, we do not propose nor recommend that the Year 2000 problem be used as a vehicle to address those weaknesses. In general, our legal system allocates economic responsibility in an equitable and legitimate manner, and to the extent that it does not do so, we do not believe that this issue presents the appropriate vehicle to implement needed changes. That said, we propose the following for consideration:

Copyright Act

Many companies seeking to upgrade their software and systems to remediate Year 2000 deficiencies are facing uncertainty, created anomalously by the U.S. Copyright Act. The Act prohibits unauthorized use, distribution, and copying of software, including creation of derivative works, unless such action is authorized by the Act (such as a "fair use" or an authorized "adaptation") or by license. Often the remedial actions required to upgrade an outdated software product are beyond the scope of the license agreement and these actions are not clearly authorized by the Copyright Act. Compounding the problem, many of the software developers and licensors are unable or unwilling to grant expansions of the license to permit this work, at least without unfairly demanding a release from liability for Year 2000 noncompliance. Other vendors cannot be located or are nonresponsive to requests for a release to perform such remediation.

This puts software users in an impossible position, and often at a stalemate with licensors and outside vendors. It could be argued that Sections 107 and/or 117 of the Copyright Act permit in-house modification of software to preserve functionality through the Year 2000. Unfortunately, there is no controlling legal precedent, and many end users and Year 2000 remediation vendors are unwilling to be the legal test case.

We propose that Congress consider modifying Section 117 of the Copyright Act, 17 U.S.C. § 117, to give legal comfort to assure end users and remediation vendors that they can employ self-help in Year 2000 remediation projects without risking substantial liability. Without such a modification, vendors are in an unfair position to obtain a release from liability and/or to demand license or other fees from users.

Safe Harbor Legislation as to Consumer Claims

We suggest that a study be undertaken to identify those Federal consumer protection laws and regulations that may be implicated as a result of a failure, by a financial institution or business, to correct a Year 2000 deficiency; and to determine if such financial institutions and business should be granted limited protection from liability for procedural violations of those laws and regulations in cases where the violations are without substantial economic harm to consumers. Any such protection should be conditioned upon the good faith pursuit of full Year 2000 remediation by the financial institution or business.

Conclusion

The ultimate goal of this Subcommittee, and those of us involved in the Year 2000 issue, is to minimize the effect of the Year 2000 problem on local, national, and international commerce. The ominous and unquantifiable threat of legal liability has compelled corporate America to acknowledge and address this issue much more aggressively than most of our international counterparts—and this is a good thing. Our experience indicates that major U.S. corporations are just now fully committing to remediate this problem, and it can be assumed that smaller business will soon follow suit. We feel that this would be an inappropriate time to relieve the pressure created by the threat of legal liability—unless that threat is either unproductive or undeserved.

PREPARED STATEMENT OF HARRIS N. MILLER

PRESIDENT, INFORMATION TECHNOLOGY ASSOCIATION OF AMERICA (ITAA)

OCTOBER 22, 1997

I am Harris Miller, President of the Information Technology Association of America, representing 11,000 direct and affiliate member companies in the information technology (IT) industry. ITAA members are the marketplace leaders in a host of critical IT areas, including product and custom software, telecommunications, Internet, systems integration, and outsourcing.

Chairman Bennett and other distinguished Members of the Subcommittee, ITAA applauds your outstanding leadership on the Year 2000 issue. The challenge we face in rising to this issue is enormous—a challenge which hits the banking and financial services community particularly hard because of:

- The information-intense, date-sensitive nature of its business.
- The forward-looking orientation of its operations.
- The immediate effect this situation could have on typical consumers.
- The risks involved in lending money to potentially unprepared customers.
- The growing reliance on electronic commerce offerings to gain competitive advantage.
- The need to interconnect with a wide variety of trading partners, both in this country and abroad.
- The enormous importance this industry represents to the national and the global economy.

ITAA supports the efforts of this Subcommittee because this is where the rubber meets the road. It will be through the efforts of this Subcommittee and others focused on key industry sectors that Year 2000 will receive the attention it deserves. We encourage similar hearings in such areas as transportation, public health, energy, defense, and other major facets of modern society.

ITAA is concerned about the Year 2000 status of both the national and the international banking system. While some national banks have staked out the high ground on this issue, I am concerned that there are many banks and financial services firms which remain silent on their Y2K preparedness. Even banks which have a Year 2000 program may be slow to translate plans into action. I am concerned that banks, like many other types of firms, are victims of analysis paralysis—the disabling disease which inhibits the ability of organizations to admit that business survival is the real issue, that mistakes will inevitably happen, and that tough choices must be made now. It's time to make those choices and move on.

From an international banking perspective, our dealings with foreign bankers suggest a disturbing degree of inaction; we hear similar concerns voiced by other observers as well. Let me offer one example. In the United States, much of the information about the Year 2000 situation travels on the Internet. The Internet plays a major role in spreading awareness, sharing comparative data, identifying candidate solutions, and the like. At a recent presentation to a meeting of Greek banks, we learned that few households in Greece are likely to have a PC, much less access to the Internet. This is just a small example of a major structural barrier to solving this problem, no doubt replicated in many—if not most—countries around the world.

Today, I have been asked to testify about ITAA's Year 2000 certification program, called ITAA*2000. I am delighted to do so, because we have a very positive story to tell. Let me begin with some brief background.

ITAA has been engaged for several years in educating governments at all levels, the private sector, and the international community about the actions necessary to address the Year 2000 and the very real risks of inaction. Last year, our Year 2000 Task Force approved the idea of a Year 2000 certification program. While the ITAA *2000 offers a substantive, rigorous technical evaluation of applicants, the program should be properly viewed from a strategic business vantage point. The topic of this hearing is liability; the focus of our program is to provide a mechanism by which organizations are able to mitigate the downstream risk associated with this work.

Other goals behind ITAA*2000 are:

- To give the marketplace a mechanism to identify the "best of breed" companies in addressing the Year 2000 issue.
- To respond to a growing sense of concern within Federal agencies and a viewpoint articulated by what was then called the Interagency Working Group that IT companies are not doing enough to respond to the Y2K compliance concerns of their customers.

- To take a proactive, industry-based stance on the Year 2000 issue, partially in response to a request made by Congressman Stephen Horn in the first Congressional hearing on this issue in April 1996.

We developed the ITAA*2000 program in conjunction with the Software Productivity Consortium (SPC) of Herndon, VA, an organization with great expertise in software process improvement. The Consortium provides the technical manpower to staff the program. We conducted a pilot to "get the bugs" out in August and September of last year, and publicly announced the program on October 1, 1996.

The program has grown to become the widely acknowledged industry certification program. I think it's fair to say that it has become something of a standard. Today, 45 organizations have received certification with another 12 in process. Several other companies have informed us they expect to submit completed applications shortly.

Let me talk briefly about one recent program graduate which is of particular interest to this body. Last month, BankBoston received ITAA*2000 certification. As you know, BankBoston has been one of the Nation's leading financial institutions in working its way through the Year 2000 thicket. As early as December 1996, we reported in our weekly *Year 2000 Outlook* publication on the impressive progress BankBoston was making with its 40-million-plus lines of code. As we said at the time, the heart of the bank's repeatable process is a sequence requiring an input, an activity, an output, a tool, and a metric. The BankBoston team applies the process to all aspects of the conversion, using iteration and yardsticks to assure that results do not go out of bounds.

That is the kind of approach which, we believe, lowers the risks involved in achieving a successful conversion. In gaining ITAA*2000 certification, BankBoston was able to demonstrate that it had a set of formal methods in place in eleven areas critical to success, from initial assessment to final testing. BankBoston is the first financial institution to gain this distinction. We hope many others will follow suit.

Almost 350 companies have requested the questionnaire necessary to submit to become certified. We are somewhat perplexed by why more completed questionnaires have not yet been submitted. Let me hazard some guesses. First, the application process is rigorous, perhaps more rigorous than some companies are willing to go through. Completed applications are often several inches thick. We do not issue these certifications lightly and some organizations fail the review. And perhaps some fail themselves, starting the process assuming it will be *pro forma* and having second thoughts when they realize the challenge of becoming certified.

There are other reasons for the relatively small response. Many companies are extremely busy talking with or servicing potential or actual Y2K customers or doing their own conversions. They simply may not have adequate staff and time to complete the questionnaire, or it may just inadvertently fall to the bottom of the "to do" list. We have talked with many companies which have assured us they are poised to submit their applications, yet have not done so, probably because of time pressure.

Let me talk for a moment about how the program works. Applicants such as BankBoston respond to an in-depth technical questionnaire, provide extensive documentation, and respond to follow-up questions. Our focus is on the processes and methods that organizations use to develop Year 2000 compliant software. To date, most of our program graduates have been information technology companies. But we have designed this program to apply to any company, Government agency, or other entity involved in Y2K conversion. The certification can involve organizations which sell products or services commercially; it can be of equal interest to those developing systems for internal use only. The certification process provides an independent, third-party review of Y2K processes and methods. Our thinking is that if you get the processes and methods right on the front end, you dramatically reduce the chances of failure down the road. This concept of reviewing processes and methods is similar to the ISO 9000 process, widely used in our industry.

We freely admit that this is not a perfect program. We have heard from some potential customers of Y2K services and products who say that because the ITAA*2000 program does not test software per se in every environment in which they use it, it fails to meet their needs. We understand their point of view, but we believe that there is still substantial value in a program which provides an independent analysis of processes and methods. ITAA*2000 certification does not offer guarantees, but it does mitigate the risks associated with this work. Organizations receiving certification demonstrate to customers, business partners, stockholders, and other interested parties that, well in advance of the century rollover, they have understood the Year 2000 problem, taken reasonable steps to correct it, and, in so doing, met the industry's best practices for dealing with the issue.

Does that mean software will operate flawlessly in the years to come? Of course not. No single industry program could hold itself out as the ultimate arbiter of Year 2000 compliance. There are simply too many platforms, systems, languages, interfaces, and other date-dependent components to check—and not enough time. Every organization's computing environment is *sui generis*. Attempting to recreate such environments on a customer-by-customer basis is just a bridge too far. The complexity and multiplicity of environments and interfaces is one reason we emphasize so strongly in our general presentations on the Year 2000 that the most time-consuming and important element of the conversion process is the testing phase. A Y2K "solution" that works very well in one computing environment may not work well at all in another environment. It simply would be impossible for us, or any organization, to test even a limited set of software products in all possible environments and interface situations.

The ITAA*2000 Certification Program should also not be considered a substitute for an organization's own verification program. For the reasons I just mentioned, we believe companies should tailor a Year 2000 verification program which is right for them—incorporating company methods and approaches, identifying key interfaces, setting testing criteria, and putting the management practices in place to ensure compliance. Part of this internal program should include steps to assure the Year 2000 compliance of hardware and software vendors, and others with products using microprocessors or programmable logic controllers. To this end, ITAA has developed a standard questionnaire for customer use in communicating with their suppliers. Our purpose is twofold: To help customers ask the right questions and to help vendors deal with the many thousands of contacts they receive on this issue, all asking for the same basic information in multiple ways.

Speaking as an IT industry executive, I am proud that ITAA has stepped up to the Year 2000 certification challenge. ITAA*2000 is one of several Year 2000 initiatives we have underway, including seminars, a Year 2000 directory, a buyer's guide, and a weekly Internet-based newsletter. We have been very active in trying to get other industries and industry groups informed about the Y2K challenge and to embrace the ITAA*2000 program. I am pleased to report that ITAA has built a collaborative Year 2000 program with the National Retail Federation. We have also briefed the Securities Industry Association, the Automotive Industry Action Council, and other groups about the program. We have also been active conference presenters on this topic at cities across the country.

And we offer ITAA*2000 overseas. I have given educational seminars around the world, including China, Singapore, Canada, France, Brazil, Mexico, and Spain. Certification is always a topic of interest. I also serve as President of the World Information Technology and Services Alliance (WITSA), comprised of 29 IT associations from around the world. WITSA has adopted a policy paper calling for an increased global focus on the Year 2000 challenge. ITAA has signed several agreements with our global sister associations to offer the certification program in their countries.

The ITAA*2000 program continues to grow and to offer important benefits to certified organizations. Today, the program enables commercial companies to set themselves apart from the competition by making a strong positive statement about their Year 2000 readiness. It allows customers to distinguish among the many vendors offering them products and services. It permits organizations to validate their own internal Year 2000 conversion processes. Tomorrow, ITAA*2000 certification program will help companies of all types mitigate risk by conclusively demonstrating that they took appropriate steps to deal with this unprecedented situation.

Thank you very much. I will be happy to respond to any questions you have about my testimony.

PREPARED STATEMENT OF BRIAN J. LANE

DIRECTOR, DIVISION OF CORPORATION FINANCE

U.S. SECURITIES AND EXCHANGE COMMISSION

OCTOBER 22, 1997

Chairman Bennett, Senator Boxer, and Members of the Subcommittee, I appreciate this opportunity to testify on behalf of the U.S. Securities and Exchange Commission ("Commission") on disclosure obligations of public companies presented by the Year 2000.

It has become increasingly apparent that a large percentage of the world's computer systems must be modified to reflect the imminent change in millennium. This includes not only internal systems of public companies, but also systems governing electronic interactions between those companies and other entities, both domestic and foreign, including suppliers, customers, creditors, borrowers, and financial services organizations.

The Commission previously reported to Congress on many aspects of the Year 2000 issues faced by public companies, the securities industry, and the Commission itself.[1] As Chairman Levitt previously testified before this Subcommittee, the Commission takes this issue very seriously, and is working, internally and with industry, to address it. This testimony will discuss just one aspect of the issue, but a very important one—disclosure by public companies.

Background

Under the Federal securities laws, disclosure is one of the principal means of protecting investors. Investors need sufficient information to make informed investment decisions—whether to buy or sell, or in some cases, whether to tender shares or how to vote. Public companies are not directly regulated by the Commission, but they must file information with the Commission on a regular basis to provide the trading markets with detailed information about their business and financial condition.[2] In the case of the Year 2000 issue, just as with any other important issue facing a company, investors need to know if there is likely to be a material financial impact on the company.

As Year 2000 began to surface as an important issue, the Commission's staff began to receive questions about the nature of public companies' disclosure obligations. Initially, the staff gave oral guidance, both to individual callers and to groups of attorneys, accountants, and business executives at conferences. As discussed below, this staff guidance emphasized the fact that disclosure of material issues was required under the Commission's current rules, and Year 2000 issues should be analyzed in the same manner as any other significant issue facing companies. This guidance was put in written form and added to the Division of Corporation Finance's *Current Issues Outline,* which is widely published in connection with conferences and available on the Commission's Web site.[3] On October 8, 1997, this guidance was formalized as Staff Legal Bulletin No. 5, which applies both to companies making filings with the Division of Corporation Finance and to investment companies and investment advisers filing with the Division of Investment Management.[4] Like all Staff Legal Bulletins, it is available on the Commission's Web site. In addition to written guidance, staff from the Divisions of Corporation Finance and Investment Management also emphasize the importance of considering the materiality of Year 2000 compliance when speaking before business people and securities practitioners.

Disclosure Requirements for Public Companies

Staff Legal Bulletin No. 5 emphasizes that companies should review, on an ongoing basis, the need to disclose costs, problems, and uncertainties associated with Year 2000 consequences. This disclosure may be required for either of two reasons: (1) there is a specific applicable disclosure requirement in the Commission's rules; or, (2) the Commission's rules require disclosure of any additional material information necessary to make the required disclosure not misleading.[5]

With respect to the specific disclosure requirements, the most significant one is the "Management's Discussion and Analysis of Financial Condition and Results of Operations" ("MD&A").[6] This item requires companies to discuss their liquidity, capital resources, results of operations, and other information necessary to an under-

---

[1] Report to Congress on the Readiness of the U.S. Securities Industry and Public Companies to Meet the Information Processing Challenges of the Year 2000 (June 1997). See also Testimony of Arthur Levitt, Chairman, U.S. Securities and Exchange Commission, Concerning the Readiness of the U.S. Securities Industry and Public Companies to Meet the Information Processing Challenges of the Year 2000 Before the Subcommittee on Financial Services and Technology of the Senate Committee on Banking, Housing, and Urban Affairs (July 30, 1997).

[2] Over 15,000 corporations and investment companies make filings with the Commission every year.

[3] The Commission's Web site is located at: http://www.sec.gov.

[4] A Staff Legal Bulletin is a statement by the Commission's staff that provides advice to the public on frequently recurring issues. It is not a statement of formal Commission position.

[5] Securities Act of 1933 Rule 408, Securities Exchange Act of 1934 Rule 12b-20, and Securities Exchange Act of 1934 Rule 14a-9. The Staff Legal Bulletin also directs filers' attention to the antifraud requirements, which apply to statements and omissions both in and outside of Commission filings. Securities Act of 1933 Section 17(a), Securities Exchange Act of 1934 Section 10(b), and Securities Exchange Act of 1934 Rule 10b-5.

[6] Item 303 of Regulations S-K and S-B. The Staff Legal Bulletin also addresses two other specific items that may elicit Year 2000 disclosure: "Description of Business" (Item 101 of Regulations S-K and S-B) and Form 8-K, the report for specified current events.

standing of a company's financial condition, changes in condition, and results of operations. As the Commission stated in its 1989 interpretive release on MD&A, the requirements are "intentionally general, reflecting the Commission's view that a flexible approach elicits more meaningful disclosure and avoids boilerplate discussions, which a more specific approach could foster." [7] Accordingly, the requirements do not specify issues that must be addressed, but rather demand that each company perform its own analysis of the issues that need to be discussed—and quantified to the extent practicable—in order for investors to assess the company and its prospects for the future. In particular, MD&A focuses on known trends, demands, commitments, events, or uncertainties that are likely to have a material impact on the company. MD&A disclosure is required in Securities Act prospectuses, as well as in annual and quarterly reports filed by public companies.

Historically, the MD&A requirement has proved to be a very useful approach to the disclosure of a variety of business or financial issues. For example, the 1989 interpretive release directs issuers' attention to the specific areas where MD&A disclosure may be appropriate, such as environmental liabilities; participation in high-yield financings, highly leveraged transactions or noninvestment grade loans and investments; the receipt by thrifts and banks of Federal financial assistance in connection with Federally assisted acquisitions or restructurings; and preliminary merger negotiations. Many other areas likely to be the subject of MD&A disclosure have been given particular attention from the Commission or its staff in the form of targeted reviews, formal or informal interpretive advice,[8] or enforcement action.[9]

The Commission believes that the Year 2000 issue, like those discussed in the interpretive release, clearly must be addressed in MD&A, to the extent it is material to a particular company. Specifically, as noted in the Staff Legal Bulletin, companies must include disclosure if either the cost of addressing the issue, or the cost of a failure to address the issue in a complete and timely manner, is likely to have a material financial impact on the company. Costs to fix Year 2000 problems may be material to a company's earnings over the next several quarters because, as the Emerging Issues Task Force decided in July 1996, they must be expensed as incurred.[10] Costs arising from a failure to correct Year 2000 problems may not be incurred until that year, but they represent for some companies today a material uncertainty that could materially affect liquidity and operating results. The requirements of MD&A call for a discussion of both types of costs, if material.

Since the MD&A approach to dealing with a variety of issues has been very successful, the staff is using the same approach to Year 2000. Companies that fail to take this requirement seriously and do not provide adequate disclosure in their Commission filings run the risk of Commission enforcement action—and, just as with the other issues discussed, the staff will be prepared to recommend instituting such action if necessary.

The current requirements are based on materiality; as a result, many companies legitimately may have no disclosure in their filings about Year 2000 issues, because they do not believe the resolution of these issues will have a material impact on the company. The Commission has considered whether specific rules are needed to require every company to make a statement about the status of its Year 2000 compliance. At this time, the Commission does not think such rules are needed. In general, the Commission's disclosure rules are premised on the philosophy that investors are best served by being provided all **material** information about a company, not by receiving affirmative statements that a particular issue is not significant for the company or is not a problem. The Commission believes the Year 2000 issues should be treated in the same manner as the other significant issues noted above. However, as discussed below, the Commission has directed both the Divisions of Corporation Finance and Investment Management to institute targeted reviews of Year 2000 dis-

---

[7] Securities Act Release No. 6835 (May 18, 1989).

[8] For example, the Commission issued an interpretive release analyzing the disclosure requirements of public companies, with particular emphasis on MD&A, to the 1988 Government investigation into illegal or unethical activity in the procurement of defense contracts. Securities Act Release No. 6791 (August 1, 1988).

[9] The Commission has instituted a number of enforcement actions involving inadequate MD&A disclosure on a variety of issues. Some examples are: The decline in New England real estate values (Bank of Boston, 1994 and 1995); the impact of the Gulf War crisis on airlines because of decreased passenger traffic and increased fuel costs (America West Airlines, 1994); and accounting for derivatives transactions (Gibson Greetings, 1995).

[10] Emerging Issues Task Force Issue No. 96–14, "Accounting for the Costs Associated with Modifying Computer Software for the Year 2000." The Emerging Issues Task Force was established in July 1984, by the Financial Accounting Standards Board to address emerging financial reporting issues.

closure. If these or subsequent reviews suggest that the current requirements are inadequate for Year 2000 issues, the Commission will reconsider this approach.

Specific Issues Involving Investment Companies and Investment Advisers

The Commission also has concluded that current laws and regulations are sufficient to require investment advisers and, in turn, the investment companies they advise, to make appropriate disclosure to clients and shareholders in the event operational or financial obstacles are presented by the Year 2000 problem.

Under the Investment Company Act of 1940, investment companies may not omit material information from registration statements and other public filings.[11] Mutual funds are required to disclose the investment adviser's experience and a brief description of the services an adviser provides.[12] In response, funds may need to disclose the effect that the Year 2000 problem would have on the adviser's ability to provide the services described in the registration statement.[13] Disclosure about the Year 2000 problem would be necessary if it would be materially misleading to shareholders to omit the information from public filings.

In addition, the Investment Advisers Act of 1940 makes it a fraudulent, deceptive, or manipulative practice for an investment adviser to fail to disclose all material facts with respect to the financial condition of the adviser that is reasonably likely to impair the ability of the adviser to meet contractual commitments to clients.[14] The pivotal determination for advisers in deciding whether disclosure is necessary in this area is whether the Year 2000 problem would materially impair the adviser's ability to satisfy its obligations under advisory agreements with investment companies and other clients. If so, disclosure of the problem to the fund board would be warranted and disclosure to shareholders may be warranted.

Similarly, case law also supports the requirement to make disclosure of material facts even in the absence of specific rules targeting the type of material information in question.[15] Therefore it is necessary, under current law, for investment advisers and investment companies alike to disclose the impact of the Year 2000 problem: (1) if there is a reasonable likelihood that the adviser will not become Year 2000 compliant in time, and (2) if there is a substantial likelihood that the Year 2000 problem would affect the adviser's ability to fulfill its contractual obligation to the investment company.

Follow-Up to Issuance of Staff Legal Bulletin

Following up on Staff Legal Bulletin No. 5, the Commission has directed the staff to take additional steps to continue focusing a high level of attention on Year 2000 disclosure. For example:

- The staff is preparing a special area of the Commission's Web site to provide useful information for both companies and investors. This will include the Staff Legal Bulletin and this testimony as well as the Commission's Report to Congress and other pronouncements and guidance in this area. This should heighten companies' attention to the disclosure requirements, as well as investors' attention to the issue—which may cause investors to focus on the information companies provide or to request additional information.
- The staff will assess disclosure regarding Year 2000 to make sure that the Staff Legal Bulletin has had its intended effect. The Division of Corporation Finance staff will focus primarily on disclosure by industries where the Year 2000 problem is most likely to have a material impact, such as the financial services industry. This will be accomplished through special reviews of filings by the companies in the selected industries, with staff members issuing comments and requesting amended filings if necessary. The reviews will begin with the disclosure in annual

---

[11] Section 34(b).

[12] Item 5(b) of Form N–1A (registration form for open-end management investment companies).

[13] Other items on Form N–1A may require disclosure of the Year 2000 problem as well. For instance, Item 4(c) calls for the disclosure of the principal risk factors associated with investing with the registrant. While this item usually relates to the risks associated with an adviser's investment practices, a discussion of the problems a fund may encounter from an adviser's inability to become Year 2000 compliant may be appropriate. Finally, disclosure of any pending legal proceedings against the fund, the adviser, or the principal underwriter relating to the Year 2000 problem would be required under Item 9; similar requirements exist for companies that file with the Division of Corporation Finance.

[14] Investment Advisers Act Rule 206(4)–4(a).

[15] Case law interpreting similar securities law provisions states that a fact is "material" if there is a substantial likelihood that a reasonable investor would consider the information important. *TSC Industries* v. *Northway, Inc.*, 426 U.S. 438, 449 (1976); *Basic, Inc.* v. *Levinson*, 485 U.S. 224, 231–32 (1988).

reports on Form 10–K or 10–KSB for companies with fiscal years ending December 31, 1997.
- Since mutual funds continuously offer their shares for sale, they are required to regularly update their prospectuses. Any material change to a fund prospectus must be filed with the Commission for review. The Division of Investment Management staff will review all fund prospectus disclosures regarding Year 2000 issues. The staff will highlight any problem areas and coordinate a review of those situations that raise concerns with the Commission's Office of Compliance Inspections and Examinations.

If the results of the reviews suggest that disclosure in this area is not satisfactory, the Divisions will consider whether to remedy the situation by increasing targeted reviews of filings on this issue, identifying ways to further educate the filing community about their disclosure obligations, or recommending that the Commission institute specific rulemaking in this area. The staff also will consider recommending that the Commission institute enforcement actions, if warranted. At present, however, the staff believes companies are attempting in good faith to understand and comply with the disclosure requirements.

Conclusion

Current laws and regulations are flexible enough to cover the reporting obligations of public companies, funds, and investment advisers regarding any material impact of Year 2000 problems. The Commission and its staff will continue to focus attention on Year 2000 disclosure to determine if any further steps are necessary. The Commission fully appreciates the importance of investor awareness of problems associated with the Year 2000, and will continue its efforts to educate filers and the public to assure that all required disclosure is complete, accurate, and timely.

PREPARED STATEMENT OF ROBERT B. AUSTRIAN
Vice President and Senior Enterprise Software Analyst
NationsBanc Montgomery Securities, Inc.

October 22, 1997

Mr. Chairman and distinguished Members of the Subcommittee, my name is Bob Austrian and I am Vice President of NationsBanc Montgomery Securities, an investment bank in San Francisco. I am a Senior Research Analyst covering the Enterprise Software Industry. In other words, my expertise is software for businesses and the vendors which supply these systems.

I appreciate the opportunity to testify before this Subcommittee and wish to note that the testimony I give today represents my personal views and does not necessarily represent the views of NationsBanc Montgomery Securities. As requested, my testimony today will be devoted to my assessment of the liability risks associated with the Year 2000 computer problem, the adequacy of disclosure in this area, and what sectors of the business community may be most vulnerable to computer failures and lawsuits resulting from the so-called "millennium bug."

Overview

First, I would like to present a brief overview of my testimony today. For the past 12 years, I have been involved in the financial, technical, and investment analysis of public companies, primarily those in the software industry. This work involves highly detailed inspection of companies' financial filings as well as other company-specific details. In addition, my colleagues and I have spent much of our time recently on the Year 2000 problem. For these reasons I believe I am qualified to comment on the adequacy of disclosure, the seriousness and uniqueness of the Year 2000 problem and its ramifications for business. I am less qualified to comment on specifics of liability, as I am not an attorney. The net conclusion from the testimony I am about to give is that I believe investors require more Year 2000-specific disclosure than is currently being provided. Our own challenge in assessing the risks faced by public companies in the Year 2000 arena is a signal that more disclosure is needed—particularly given that we are "experts" in this area. The risk is both greater and faster changing than most other risks companies face.

Background

I am an investment analyst providing technology, financial, and investment analysis of the companies that provide software solutions for businesses. Some of these companies provide solutions to the Year 2000 problem. I have 12 years experience following public companies in the software sector. My colleagues, of whom one, Tom Pagel, is here with me today, and I have been researching the Year 2000 issue in-depth throughout this year and have been watching the issue unfold for some time. In September, we published what we believe is a fairly detailed, investment-focused report on the matter. We have distributed a copy of our report, entitled "Millennium Morass," along with this prepared statement. As part of our background research for the "Millennium Morass" report, we surveyed 67 technology managers, inter-viewed scores of managers, including a number of senior managers in Fortune 500-class companies, and reviewed a wealth of published material on the subject.

Our Perspective on the Year 2000 Problem

We believe the Year 2000 problem is significant, but will not bring about the end of "life as we know it" (as some doomsayers are predicting). We think worldwide in-formation technology (IT) expenditures to address and fix (whenever possible) the problem will total at least $600 billion. Importantly, this figure does not include liti-gation expenses, which we believe will be significant. As described in the accom-panying report, we believe there is no longer enough time for all organizations to fix the problem, assuming manual (versus tools-based, automation-assisted) tech-niques are used. Even with the use of software tools to automate part of the task of fixing this problem, we believe many organizations, including the Federal Govern-ment, may fail to make all of their systems compliant in time.

The Year 2000 problem is a unique example of an IT challenge, unlike any other IT issue ever encountered. A number of factors differentiate the Year 2000 problem from other IT issues. Our "Millennium Morass" report includes detailed descriptions of these factors, which are outlined here. First, the problem affects virtually all com-panies. Second, it affects them simultaneously. Third, the deadline for completion of the project will not move. Fourth, the deadline is unrelated to the size of the task. And last, the deadline is much earlier than expected for many applications. We be-lieve the net result of these factors, together with an already constrained technology labor supply, is a shortage of two key resources: Time and labor. We stress that money is not necessarily in short supply within organizations, and that, given time constraints, spending additional money will not solve the problem alone. In short, there is a bona fide shortage of time and labor, and the situation is worsening al-most daily. We believe most large organizations, especially those currently in the earliest stages of addressing the problem, will be extremely challenged to complete the job on time. Many will "triage" and fix only the most critical systems. We believe it is likely that the Federal Government will not complete even its so-called "mis-sion-critical" systems on time. Note that "on-time" does not mean by January 1, 2000, but rather some date between today and January 1, 2000, as most software systems "look ahead" by some amount of time as, say, a calendar program on your PC plans a year at a time.

Status Report

As of today, there are exactly 800 days remaining until January 1, 2000. We be-lieve the vast majority of companies have begun to address the issue in some way, although most (at least 70 percent) are still in the earliest "assessment" phase, now determining the size and scope of their task. A small but growing group of compa-nies have disclosed their cost estimates. Expected investments of $40 million or more are common within the Global 3000, and several companies have estimated that they will spend $200 million or more in this area. Federal Government agencies now estimate that they will spend $3.8 billion, up from an initial estimate of $2.3 billion early this year. External sources estimate that the Government's tab will be as high as $30 billion.

Liability Risks Associated with the Year 2000 Problem

While we are not attorneys, we believe organizations and their officers face poten-tial liability in many areas. For example, companies that do not fully disclose the dimensions of their Year 2000 problems may be liable under Federal securities laws. Our research has led us to consider a few additional examples. Companies (in many industries) selling products that are not "Year 2000 compliant" and cause financial or other damage to the buyer may be liable. Examples include vendors of software or any products with "embedded technology," such as computers, elevators, auto-mobiles, etc. Financial institutions that lose track of account balances or fail to exe-cute transactions properly may be liable. "Year 2000 companies" that supply tools or services to fix Year 2000 problems may be liable if "repaired" software is not fixed properly. Finally, companies may be liable for damages experienced by their corporate customers. For example, manufacturing "supply chain" companies could be liable if their systems fail and do not adequately supply products. With respect to this topic, we cite the following communication, reported in March 1997, by an industry trade group, Information Technology Association of America (ITAA):

> An executive trio from the Big Three automakers urged the industry's supplier community to get on with their Y2K assessments. A letter signed by T.T. Stallkamp, Executive Vice President, Chrysler Corp.; C.E. Mazzorin, Vice President, Ford Motor Co.; and H.R. Kutner, Vice President, General Motors, to over 10,000 production and nonproduction supplier companies describes the Year 2000 situation and notes, "Problems associated with the Year 2000 have already occurred in some of our systems and will continue to occur before January 1, 2000, as applications start using Year 2000 and beyond dates. Your company is probably starting to be affected also or will be shortly. The consequences, if not dealt with quickly and effectively, can jeopardize your company's very ability to operate." The executives inform their suppliers that, through the Automotive Industry Action Group of Southfield, Michigan, they are developing supplier management awareness briefings and a common approach to supplier Y2K certification.

To summarize, we believe there are many areas of potential liability for organizations, including many beyond those described here. As we are not experts on legal matters, we offer only limited discussion and a few examples we have encountered or considered during our research.

Adequacy of Disclosure in this Area
Current Disclosure Requirements and Examples

Currently, companies are required to address Year 2000 issues that are material to investors in their SEC filings. While all companies have some Year 2000 exposure—we believe it is material for many—few have addressed the issue in their filings. Of those that have, the vast majority state either that it is not a material issue, or that they do not know how large the problem is. A small percentage estimate what it will cost to make needed repairs. Below are a few examples (edited for brevity) of what companies have stated in recent SEC filings:

- "As of December 31, 1996, the company has identified a majority of its computer systems that are not 'Year 2000' compliant. It is not expected that modifying or replacing these systems will have a material effect in 1997 on the company's financial statements taken as a whole." Dow Jones & Co., Inc., FY 1996 10–K
- "Citicorp, like other companies, is in the process of assessing and repairing its computer applications to ensure functionality with respect to the 'Year 2000' millennium change. At present, Citicorp does not anticipate that material incremental costs will be incurred in any single future year." Citicorp, FY 1996 10–K
- "FSCO is expending significant resources to assure that its computer systems are reprogrammed in time to effectively deal with transactions in the Year 2000 and beyond. This will have a material impact on FSCO's ability to conduct its business, and especially to process and account for the transfer of funds electronically." First Security Corporation, FY 1996 10–K
- "The total cost of compliance and its effect on the Company's future results of operation is being determined as part of the detailed conversion planning." Ford Motor Co., FY 1996 10–K
- "The Company has been modifying its computer systems to address this issue. However, due to the interdependent nature of computer systems, the Company may be adversely impacted in the Year 2000 depending on whether it or other entities not affiliated with the Company address this issue successfully." Morgan Stanley, FY 1996 10–K

More Detailed Disclosure Needed

We believe more detailed disclosure is needed than has been provided to date. As a result of the uniqueness and seriousness of the problem, we believe investors should be provided with more practicable and specific information about this area of risk than other, more general areas and types of risk. Conveying to investors that say, "expenditures required to fix the problem are material" or are "not material" does not adequately represent a corporation's risk to investors. Such minimal or general purpose disclosures fail to adequately reflect the probability or associated risk of not complying on time. The following factors demonstrate why we believe the situation is now serious enough for special treatment.

Companies, in general, are seriously behind schedule in achieving compliance. Assuming software applications actually process "look-ahead" dates of up to 1 year in advance, compliant applications should be fully implemented by the end of 1998, and testing should, therefore, begin by the end of 1997. However, companies are still mostly in assessment. An August 1997 poll of 128 Fortune 500 IT directors and managers by Rubin Systems Inc. for Year 2000 services provider Cap Gemini revealed that only 16 percent have begun implementing a full-fledged strategy and only 24 percent have a detailed plan in place.

In addition, expenses will be material. We believe the average Fortune 500 company will spend at least $100 million on its fix. Chase Manhattan, Merrill Lynch, Hughes Electronics, and Prudential have all publicly stated that they will each spend at least $100 million on the problem.

However, more important than monetary expenditures are risks associated with shortages of time and labor resources. This perspective is not yet broadly embraced, and disclosures about "risk" in this area similarly under-emphasize these critical factors. We believe that financially, most organizations will not be too negatively affected by the Year 2000 problem, but that many may literally run out of time and labor resources. Specifically, there is a serious shortage of labor that is only getting worse. Estimates of the number of incremental programmers needed to address the problem in the United States range from 150,000 to 200,000 or more. These needs exist against the backdrop of an industry-wide base of less than 2,000,000 programmers, all of whom were recently fully employed on projects other than the Year 2000. In April, Gartner Group reported that 1997 labor costs rose 30 percent from 1996 (when they averaged $60 per hour) and are still climbing. We believe labor costs for skilled IT personnel will continue to increase at least 30 percent per year over the next 3 years.

What Should be Disclosed

To most fully understand the Year 2000 problem's effect on an organization, we believe investors should be provided with:

- Estimated amounts and timing of direct costs (comprised of labor, software, and hardware investments).
- Liability risks and their respective probabilities.
- High-level quantified assessments of systems that need to be fixed.
- Schedules for achieving compliance.

In addition, there should be quarterly reporting of milestones completed relative to plan, as well as new risks recently encountered. Some may respond that in order to gather these details, investors can simply ask. We attempted exactly that in March 1997, when we surveyed 5,000 senior technology managers in U.S. corporations. Only 1.3 percent (67) of our surveys were returned, demonstrating what we believe is an unwillingness to disclose facts concerning progress or the lack thereof on addressing this issue. Finally, it is not surprising that senior corporate managers have been unwilling to discuss this matter on the record: Few are ahead of the game. If more were on track with efforts to remedy any deficiencies, we would be hearing more about it, as success in addressing the issue would quickly become a competitive differentiator.

Software Companies May Require Special Treatment

The software companies may be unique with respect to Year 2000-related risk. They may be subject to: (1) exaggerated demand for software products in one period—i.e., as Year 2000 replacements are undertaken—followed by periods of lower growth thereafter; and, (2) re-allocation of spending away from new IT projects in favor of fixing Year 2000 legacy code. For example, one of the leading software companies in this country, Oracle Corporation, recently filed a 10–K that includes the following:

> . . . industry analysts have noted that a significant amount of current demand for applications software is generated by customers in the process of replacing and upgrading applications not designed to automatically accommodate the change in date from December 31, 1999 to January 1, 2000. Once such customers have completed their preparations for the Year 2000, the software industry and the Company may experience a significant deceleration from the strong annual growth rates recently experienced in the applications software marketplace.

In addition, earlier this month, *PC Week* magazine quoted leading software vendor PeopleSoft's CEO Dave Duffield at a Gartner Group symposium:

> The [spending] boom is gone because of Year 2000 spending. And that could result in a major slowdown of deployments.

We expect to see similar disclosures from other software companies that are currently experiencing increased, but temporary, demand as a result of the Year 2000 issue. Some factors we believe affect the respective levels of risk among software companies include the extent to which their applications replace the existing, noncompliant systems and the amount of time required to install such products. We believe these topics should be addressed by software companies, whether they are required to do so or not.

Industries Most Vulnerable to Failures and Lawsuits in the Year 2000

We believe that nearly all sectors of the business community are vulnerable to the Year 2000 problem. Some are more vulnerable than others, including those with the most date-intensive applications. These include banking, investments, insurance, and manufacturing industries, the latter more a result of their highly computer-dependent, "just-in-time" inventory practices than of a high incidence of dates *per se*.

In December 1996, International Data Corporation surveyed 500 executives of medium and large companies spanning six industries including banking, insurance, investing, manufacturing, utilities, and communications. Executives in the banking, insurance, and investing industries stated most frequently that the possibility of legal liabilities existed in their industries; 55 percent, 43 percent, and 37 percent, respectively, responded "Yes" to "Possibility of legal liabilities arising from Y2K problems?" In the survey, the following sources of legal challenge were named by the percentages of executives shown (more than one answer was allowed): Customers—62 percent. Regulators—32 percent. Stockholders/Policyholders—21 percent. Suppliers—3 percent. Other/Don't Know—18 percent.

Although some industries seem more likely to experience legal liability than others, we strongly believe that all industries are affected by the problem and subject to litigation risk. Thus, with the possible exception of the software industry described above, we do not believe it is useful to distinguish among industries in terms of regulation or disclosure requirements with respect to the Year 2000 issue.

Summary

We believe the Year 2000 problem is both real and large. Organizations need, and are only now increasingly securing, involvement from CEO's; we believe this is necessary for organizations to have a sophisticated and credible approach to the problem and to boost the probability that they achieve timely compliance. We stress that the greatest danger for management is to look only at monetary costs to fix the problem, which in many cases do not appear significant as a percentage of the organization's revenues. Focusing on monetary costs can obscure the significant shortages of time and labor resources that can and do exist. These shortages cannot be adequately addressed by higher spending. This critical point can be easily missed by those with limited experience in information technology or an overemphasis on financial burden and financial risk. We hope that organizational management will understand the issue and devote the necessary attention to solve the problem. Finally, we believe the Federal Government faces as much risk as any organization. Just as any company's CEO should be involved in addressing these issues, attention from the President may be required to achieve satisfactory results.

Mr. Chairman and distinguished Members of the Subcommittee, that concludes my testimony and I would be happy to entertain any questions you may have.

United States General Accounting Office

GAO

Testimony

For the Subcommittee on Financial Services and Technology, Committee on Banking, Housing, and Urban Affairs, U.S. Senate

For Release
at 10 a.m.
Wednesday,
October 22, 1997

YEAR 2000 COMPUTING CRISIS

National Credit Union Administration's Efforts to Ensure Credit Union Systems Are Year 2000 Compliant

Statement for the Record by
Jack L. Brock, Jr.
Director, Information Resources Management/
   General Government Issues
Accounting and Information Management Division

Mr. Chairman and Members of the Subcommittee:

We are pleased to be asked to provide our views on the progress being made by the National Credit Union Administration (NCUA) in ensuring that automated information systems belonging to the thousands of credit unions that NCUA oversees are ready for the upcoming century date change. If the Year 2000 problem is not addressed in time, credit union computer systems—which affect billions of dollars of assets and transactions—will be unable to readily process transactions or produce accurate information. According to NCUA, without properly functioning systems, credit unions like other financial institutions face the potential of failure.

This testimony is the first in a series of reports you requested on the status of efforts by federal financial regulatory agencies to ensure that the organizations they oversee are ready to handle the Year 2000 computer conversion challenge. To prepare for this testimony, we performed a quick overview of NCUA's efforts to date to ensure that credit unions have adequately mitigated the risks associated with the Year 2000 date change and compared these activities to our Year 2000 Assessment Guide.[1] In performing the overview, we interviewed NCUA officials responsible for examining and overseeing the safety and soundness of credit union management practices and procedures. We reviewed examination policies, procedures, and manuals—including specific examination procedures for assessing Year 2000 compliance. We also reviewed NCUA correspondence to credit unions and third-party contractors (that provide automated systems services to many credit unions) regarding the Year 2000 problem. Finally, we interviewed officials from the Credit Union National Association, the National Association of State Credit Union Supervisors, and the CUNA Mutual Group (which provides liability insurance for the credit union industry). We provided a draft of this testimony to NCUA for review and comment. NCUA officials stated that they would provide written comments at a later date. We performed our work at NCUA headquarters in Alexandria, Virginia, between October 7 and 17, 1997, in accordance with generally accepted government auditing standards.

---

[1] Year 2000 Computing Crisis: An Assessment Guide (GAO/AIMD-10.1.14, September 1997). Published as a exposure draft in February 1997 and finalized in September 1997, the guide was issued to help federal agencies prepare for the Year 2000 conversion. It addresses common issues affecting most federal agencies and presents a structured approach and a checklist to aid in planning, managing, and evaluating Year 2000 programs. The guide describes five phases—supported by program and project management activities—with each phase representing a major Year 2000 program activity or segment. While the guide focuses on federal agencies, it is general enough that nonfederal organizations can also use it to assess their automated systems.

As requested, my testimony today will highlight the Year 2000 problem's potential impact on credit unions and their systems. I will then discuss NCUA's Year 2000 strategy and highlight our observations with its efforts to ensure that credit unions are appropriately addressing the problem.

In summary, we found that the Year 2000 problem poses a serious dilemma for credit unions because they like other financial institutions rely heavily on information systems. We also found that NCUA recognizes the severity of the problem, has developed a plan, and has initiated action. For example, NCUA issued several letters to the credit unions informing them of the risks associated with Year 2000 problem. In addition, working in conjunction with other federal financial regulators, NCUA developed procedures for examiners to use in reviewing credit union Year 2000 efforts. However, we are concerned with NCUA's approach because (1) current agency efforts to determine industrywide compliance are behind the generally accepted schedule for achieving Year 2000 compliance, and, consequently, NCUA does not yet have a complete picture of where credit unions stand individually or as an industry, (2) the agency lacks a formal, documented contingency plan in case credit unions do not become compliant in time or have other problems, (3) credit union internal auditors may not be thoroughly addressing Year 2000 issues as part of their work, and (4) NCUA does not have enough technical capability to conduct Year 2000 and other examinations in complex systems areas.

The Year 2000 Problem Poses a Serious Dilemma for Credit Unions

Credit unions are nonprofit financial cooperatives organized to provide their members with low-cost financial services. According to NCUA, as of 1996, federally insured credit union assets totaled $326 billion. About one in four Americans belongs to a credit union, and credit unions accounted for about 2 percent of the total financial services in the United States.

NCUA supervises and insures more than 7,200 federally chartered credit unions and insures member deposits in an additional 4,200 state-chartered credit unions through the National Credit Union Share Insurance Fund. As part of its goal of maintaining the safety and soundness of the credit unions, NCUA is responsible for ensuring credit unions are addressing the Year 2000 problem.

The Year 2000 problem is rooted in the way dates are recorded and computed in automated information systems. For the past several decades, systems have typically used two digits to represent the year, such as "97" representing 1997, in order to conserve on electronic data storage and reduce operating costs. With this two-digit format, however, the year 2000 is indistinguishable from 1900, or 2001 from 1901. As a result of this ambiguity, system or application programs that use dates to perform calculations, comparisons, or sorting may generate incorrect results.

According to NCUA, most credit unions rely on computers to provide for processing and updating of records and a variety of other functions. As such, the Year 2000 problem poses a serious dilemma for the industry. For example, the problem could lead to numerous problems when calculations requiring the use of dates are performed, such as calculating interest, calculating truth-in-lending or truth-in-savings disclosures, and determining amortization schedules. Moreover, automated teller machines may also assume that all bank cards are expired due to this problem. In addition, errors caused by Year 2000 miscalculations may expose institutions and data centers to financial liability and risk of damage to customer confidence. Other systems important to the day-to-day business of credit unions may be affected as well. For example, telephone systems could shut down as can vaults, security and alarm systems, elevators, and fax machines.

In addressing the Year 2000 problem, credit unions must also consider the computer systems that interface with, or connect to, their own systems. These systems may belong to payment system partners, such as wire transfer systems, automated clearing houses, check clearing providers, credit card merchant and issuing systems, automated teller machine networks, electronic data interchange systems, and electronic benefits transfer systems. Because these systems are also vulnerable to the Year 2000 problem, they can introduce and/or propagate errors into credit unions systems. Accordingly, credit unions must develop comprehensive solutions to this problem and prevent unintentional consequences from affecting their systems and the systems of others.

To address these Year 2000 challenges, GAO issued its Year 2000 Assessment Guide[2] to help federal agencies plan, manage, and evaluate their efforts. The Office of Management and Budget (OMB), which is responsible for developing the Year 2000 strategy for federal agencies, also issued similar guidance. Both require a structured approach to planning and managing five delineated phases of an effective Year 2000 program. The phases include (1) raising awareness of the problem, (2) assessing the complexity and impact the problem can have on systems, (3) renovating, or correcting, systems, (4) validating, or testing, corrections, and

---

[2]GAO/AIMD-10.1.14, September 1997.

(5) implementing corrected systems. GAO has also identified other dimensions to solving the Year 2000 problem, such as identifying interfaces with outside organizations and their systems and establishing agreements with these organizations specifying how data will be exchanged in the year 2000 and beyond. In addition, GAO and OMB have established a timeline for completing each of the five phases and believe agencies should have completed assessment phase activities last summer and should be well into renovation with the goal of completing this phase by mid to late 1998. Our work at other federal agencies indicates that because the cost of systems failures can be very high, contingency plans must be prepared so that core business functions will continue to be performed even if systems have not been made Year 2000 compliant.

NCUA Has Developed a Strategy and Has Initiated Action to Address the Year 2000 Problem

NCUA has developed a three-pronged approach for ensuring that credit unions are aggressively addressing the Year 2000 problem, which encompasses (1) incorporating the Year 2000 issue into its examination and supervision program, (2) disseminating information about the problem to credit unions, and (3) assessing Year 2000 compliance on the part of credit union data processing vendors.

The first aspect of NCUA's strategy, the examination and supervision program, involves assessing credit union Year 2000 efforts through regular annual examinations at the 7,200 federally chartered credit unions and 30 to 40 percent of the 4,200 federally insured, state chartered credit unions for which NCUA conducts an insurance review. These examinations seek to identify credit unions that are in danger of not renovating their systems on time and to reach "formal agreements" that specify corrective measures. In conducting these reviews, examiners are to follow NCUA guidelines, which provide step-by-step procedures for identifying problem areas. Once a formal agreement is reached, the examiner is expected to monitor the credit union's implementation of the agreed-upon corrective measures. Also as part of its examination effort, NCUA has contracted a consulting firm to train selected examiners in Year 2000 efforts. Through this training, NCUA expects to have one in-house Year 2000 specialist available as a resource for every eight examiners. In addition, NCUA's board recently authorized the hiring of an electronic data processing (EDP) auditor to provide more in-depth technical assistance and education on Year 2000 problems.

Another part of NCUA's examination and supervision strategy includes working with state regulators to ensure that federally insured, state chartered credit unions are also Year 2000 compliant. Officials from NCUA and the National Association of State Credit Union Supervisors told us that all but two state regulators are following the same Year 2000 examination strategy established by NCUA; the other two state regulators are planning on performing added steps in addition to performing those included in NCUA's strategy.

The second aspect of NCUA's strategy—information dissemination—seeks to heighten credit union awareness of the Year 2000 problem. In August 1996 and June 1997 letters to federally insured credit unions, NCUA formally alerted credit unions to the potential dangers of the Year 2000 problem, identified the specific impacts the problem could have on the industry, provided detailed explanations of the problem, and identified steps needed to correct the problem. It also related its plans to include Year 2000 evaluations in regular examinations and provided credit unions with copies of its examination guidance. In addition, NCUA has appointed a Year 2000 executive responsible for achieving Year 2000 compliance industrywide and assigned Year 2000 compliance officers to its central office and six regional offices. These staff will be responsible for serving as Year 2000 focal points to coordinate efforts across the agency. Finally, NCUA is working with credit union trade groups, such as the Credit Union National Association, in raising awareness of Year 2000 issues.

The third component of NCUA's program—vendor compliance—targets organizations that provide electronic data processing services to credit unions. According to NCUA, approximately 40 vendors provide data processing services to 76 percent of all federally insured credit unions, which account for 79 percent of federally insured credit union assets. Consequently, it is vital that these vendors correct their own systems and help ensure that information can be easily transferred after the Year 2000 deadline. NCUA has begun identifying and contacting major EDP vendors, and it plans to assess their efforts through questionnaires. Specifically, in May 1997 and again in August 1997, NCUA mailed a questionnaire to the 87 vendors, including the 40 vendors that support the bulk of credit unions, requesting information on Year 2000 readiness and, as of September 1997, had received 29 responses.

Concerns With NCUA's Year 2000 Efforts

While NCUA has initiated actions to build the Year 2000 issue into examinations and to raise awareness about the issue among credit unions and their vendors, our work to date has identified four issues that must be addressed to provide greater assurance that NCUA efforts will be successful.

First and foremost of our concerns is that NCUA still does not have a complete picture of where credit unions and their vendors stand in resolving the Year 2000 problem, and current efforts to determine credit union compliance are behind the schedule established by OMB and GAO. To collect information from the credit unions on their Year 2000 status, NCUA examiners used a high-level questionnaire that inquired whether (1) credit union systems were capable and ready to handle Year 2000 processing, (2) plans were in place to resolve the problem, (3) enough funds were budgeted to correct systems, and (4) responsibility and reporting mechanisms were appropriately established to support the Year 2000 effort. NCUA issued a separate high-level questionnaire to credit union vendors. However, as of the time of our work, NCUA had not yet queried 20 percent of the credit unions and had only received 29 of the 87 vendor responses. In addition, of the credit union and vendor responses received, NCUA has not yet analyzed the information to determine which credit unions and vendors are at high risk of not correcting their systems on time.

This problem is compounded by the fact that the NCUA questionnaires did not inquire about the status of efforts in completing each important phase of correction: (1) raising awareness of the problem, (2) assessing the complexity and impact the problem can have on systems, (3) renovating, or correcting, systems, (4) validating, or testing, corrections, and (5) implementing corrected systems. The questionnaires also did not include system interface issues. For example, they did not inquire about (1) identifying interfaces with outside organizations and their systems, such as payment, check clearing, credit card, and benefit transfer systems, and (2) establishing agreements with these organizations specifying how data will be exchanged in the year 2000 and beyond.

As a result, even when NCUA assesses the results, it still will not have a complete understanding of how far along the industry is in addressing the problem. In addition, NCUA examinations are conducted only on an annual basis. This means that each credit union will be examined only two more times between the end of 1997 and the year 2000. Further, NCUA has not yet established a formal mechanism for credit unions to submit interim progress reports to provide an up-to-date picture of individual correction efforts between examinations. NCUA officials told us that examiners perform off-site supervision in between exams by tracking performance via credit union financial reports and by contacting credit union officials should a problem arise. However, this may not be enough given the seriousness of the problem and the fact that the Year 2000 deadline is just 2 years away.

Further complicating NCUA's situation is the fact that it is still involved in assessment phase activities. According to OMB and GAO guidance, these activities should have been completed back in the summer. As it stands, NCUA does not plan to complete them until the end of this calendar year.

Accordingly, we believe NCUA should accelerate agency efforts to complete the assessment of the state of the industry by no later than November 15, 1997, rather than waiting until the end of the year. NCUA should also collect the necessary information to determine the exact phase of each credit union and vendor in addressing the Year 2000 problem. Because NCUA currently does not have a process in place for interim reporting of this information between examinations, NCUA should require credit unions to report the precise status (phase) of their efforts on at least a quarterly basis. One option would be to use the financial reports, commonly referred to as call reports, that credit unions provide to NCUA quarterly. As part of this report, NCUA should also require credit unions to report on the status of identifying their interfaces to determine whether this issue is being adequately addressed and, if not, require credit unions to implement such agreements as soon as possible.

A second concern we have with NCUA's efforts is that the agency does not yet have a formal contingency plan. Our <u>Year 2000 Assessment Guide</u>[3] calls on agencies to initiate realistic contingency plans during the assessment phase for critical systems to ensure the continuity of their core business processes. Contingency planning is important because it identifies alternative activities, which may include manual and contract procedures, to be employed should systems fail to meet the Year 2000 deadline. NCUA guidance directs credit unions to conduct contingency planning, and NCUA officials told us that they have developed numerous contingency options and have discussed among the staff what steps to take should a credit union not be compliant by January 1, 2000. However, officials stated that the precise actions have not been documented in a formal plan. Not having this plan increases the risk of unnecessary problems in an already uncertain situation. Consequently, we recommend that NCUA formally document its contingency plans.

---

[3]GAO/AIMD-10.1.14, September 1997.

A third concern that we have is that credit union auditors may not be addressing the Year 2000 problem as part of their work. NCUA requires each credit union to perform supervisory committee audits. These audits are to determine whether management practices and procedures are sufficient to safeguard members' assets and whether effective internal controls are in place to guard against error, carelessness, and fraud. They are conducted by the credit union's supervisory committee staff or by an outside accountant. However, NCUA officials noted that such reviews typically focus on general controls (e.g., ensuring accurate data is entered into the system, securing data from unauthorized use) and would not specifically include controls to prevent malfunctions due to the Year 2000 problem. Audits are an integral management control and expanding their scope to include important and high-risk Year 2000 issues is critical since it would provide credit union management with greater assurance and understanding about where their institution stands in addressing the problem.

Accordingly, we are recommending to NCUA that it require credit unions to implement the necessary management controls to ensure that these financial institutions have adequately mitigated the risks associated with the Year 2000 problem. Specifically, NCUA should require credit union auditors to include Year 2000 issues within the scope of their management and internal control work and report serious problems and corrective actions to NCUA immediately. To aid credit union auditors in this effort, NCUA should provide the auditors with the procedures developed by NCUA for its examiners to use in assessing Year 2000 compliance and any other guidance that would be instructive.

We also believe NCUA should require credit unions to establish processes whereby credit union management would be responsible for certifying Year 2000 readiness by a deadline well before the millennium. Such a certification process should include credit union compliance testing by an independent third party and should allow sufficient time for NCUA to review the results.

Our fourth concern is that NCUA does not have enough staff qualified to conduct examination work in complex technical areas. At present, NCUA is the process of hiring one EDP auditor to help examine thousands of credit unions. Recognizing this weakness, NCUA is considering hiring up to three EDP auditors. However, these personnel additions may still not suffice given the tremendous workload and the short time frame for getting it done. To mitigate this concern, we recommend that before the end of the year, NCUA determine the level of technical capability needed to allow for thorough review of credit unions' Year 2000 efforts and hire or contract for this capability.

Summary

Our initial work showed that NCUA has made some progress in addressing Year 2000 compliance issues for credit unions systems that it regulates. However, we are concerned that NCUA (1) is behind schedule and does not yet know the exact status of credit union Year 2000 readiness, (2) has not prepared a formal, detailed plan for contingencies, (3) does not have assurance that sufficient credit union management controls are in place to address Year 2000 problems, and (4) is lacking sufficient technical capability. These concerns lead us to believe that NCUA needs to do more to ensure that credit unions have adequately mitigated the risks associated with the Year 2000 problem, and we have made recommendations to assist NCUA in addressing these issues.

APEX

TP_CF

76523826 — 22